What People Are Saying About James Goll and *Passionate Pursuit*...

I have seen firsthand how people experience freedom and a new beginning when they personally receive the love and blessing of the heavenly Father in their lives. Author James Goll describes how to enter into this reality as he unfolds a truth we must embrace for our spiritual well-being: We have a heavenly Father who wants us to know Him intimately. He calls us to pursue Him passionately and to allow Him to lead us step-by-step into His presence. *Passionate Pursuit* reveals in a fresh way that God the Father desires to bless His children—and that our greatest blessing from the Father is to know Him and be known by Him.

—*Michael W. Smith*
Singer, songwriter, and author

Passionate Pursuit: Getting to Know God and His Word by James Goll is an incredibly refreshing book. Whether you are a new believer struggling to learn where to start in knowing God and His Word or a seasoned saint who has read the Bible many times over, this book offers you the most beautiful gift: an introduction and reintroduction to your First Love. The author personifies the title of this book—*Passionate Pursuit*. If ever I have met someone who models that phrase, it would be James Goll. James leads you past where you may have felt limitations or blockages in the Word and invites you into the ease and beauty of knowing God through the Scriptures. He invites you into his personal life and how he encounters the God of the Scriptures. In doing so, he provides you with vital tools for knowing God and His Word. This book will fill you with hope and encouragement as you approach the simplicity of knowing God and knowing Him through His Word, the Bible.

—*Bill Johnson*
Bethel Church, Redding, California
Author, *When Heaven Invades Earth*

James Goll writes on how to embark on a lifelong adventure that begins with establishing a personal connection with the heavenly Father and progresses with an ever-deepening knowledge of Him. If you've ever wondered if it's really possible to encounter the living God, read this book. *Passionate Pursuit* will help you walk through a process of personal transformation as you experience the heart of God, draw close to Him, and grow to be a living example of His very nature and life.

—*Mike Bickle*
Director, International House of Prayer of Kansas City

James Goll has blessed the church with a wealth of revelation in the many books he has written. He now brings to us his latest masterpiece, *Passionate Pursuit: Getting to Know God and His Word.* You will gain a deeper revelation of who God is, as Father, Son, and Holy Spirit, as well as who you are in Him. You will be biblically anchored and spiritually enlightened. I highly recommend this book, which will set you ablaze on a holy, passionate pursuit after Jesus, the Lover of your soul!

—*Dr. Ché Ahn*
Apostle, Harvest Apostolic Center, Pasadena, California
Senior Pastor, HRock Church
President, Harvest International Ministry
International Chancellor, Wagner Leadership Institute

Passionate Pursuit will cause you to fall more deeply in love with God. For those of you who have gone tepid in the faith, this book will cause you to burn with an abandoned passion for God. For those of you who are seeking new depths with Him, dive into this book!

—*Cindy Jacobs*
Cofounder, Generals International
Dallas, Texas

If you know James Goll at all, or have read any of his books, you know this about him: He is a man who pursues God with everything in him…heart, soul, mind, and body. His new book, *Passionate Pursuit*, offers living water from the Word for the thirsting soul on a journey to know God more. It's filled with such solid, foundational truth about who God is, it will no doubt become a classic. If you know someone new to the kingdom, be sure to give them a copy, but before you do, read it yourself and be blessed!

—*Jane Hansen Hoyt*
President/CEO
Aglow International

Are you hungry to really know God? Are you aware deep within your soul that God is an outrageously loving Father who passionately has, does, and will pursue you? When you read this lively book, *Passionate Pursuit*, it might just create a desire in you to thirst for God like the deer pants for the water brooks. If you want to experience a "burning heart," as the two disciples did on the road to Emmaus (see Luke 24:32)—and not just grow in head knowledge about another "religion"—allow my friend James Goll to ignite the fire of passion within you so you can come to know your amazing, creator God.

—*Mickey Robinson*
Founder, Prophetic Destiny International
Author, *Falling into Heaven*

Years ago, as I began to realize that the church was devoid of the prophet's voice, I invited James Goll to Nashville. By that time, I was acquainted with many of those with strong prophetic ministries, but James' voice was one that I trusted. I still trust that voice. James has made me jealous for more of Jesus. I am honored to be considered one of his spiritual fathers, and I can guarantee you that this book, *Passionate Pursuit: Getting to Know God and His Word*, will challenge you to draw nearer to God and to His Word. Grab this book and get ready to have Holy Spirit fire torched into your bones.

—*Dr. Don Finto*
Founder, The Caleb Company, Nashville, Tennessee
Author, *Your People Shall Be My People*

PASSIONATE Pursuit

JAMES W. GOLL

WHITAKER
HOUSE

PASSIONATE PURSUIT:
Getting to Know God and His Word

James W. Goll
Encounters Network
P.O. Box 1653 • Franklin, TN 37065
www.encountersnetwork.com • www.prayerstorm.com
www.compassionacts.com • www.GETeSchool.com
info@encountersnetwork.com • inviteJames@gmail.com

ISBN: 978-1-62911-277-0 • eBook ISBN: 978-1-62911-278-7
Printed in the United States of America
© 2015 by James W. Goll

Whitaker House
1030 Hunt Valley Circle
New Kensington, PA 15068
www.whitakerhouse.com

Library of Congress Cataloging-in-Publication Data

Goll, Jim W.
  Passionate pursuit : getting to know God and his word / James W. Goll.
     pages cm
  Includes bibliographical references.
  ISBN 978-1-62911-277-0 (trade pbk. : alk. paper) – ISBN 978-1-62911-278-7 (ebook)
  1. God (Christianity)—Knowableness. I. Title.
  BT103.G653 2015
  231—dc23
                              2014041599

1 2 3 4 5 6 7 8 9 10 11 ⨄ 22 21 20 19 18 17 16 15

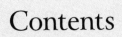

Contents

Acknowledgments and Dedication

I am indebted to a number of key leaders who have impacted my life over the years. I have often mentioned the immeasurable teaching imprint that Derek Prince had on my life at an early age. His fingerprints are still all over me. Much later in my journey, I had the joy and honor of working with Mike Bickle, of the now-famous International House of Prayer of Kansas City. I have never met anyone who, over a protracted period of time, has exhibited a greater passion for Jesus than this man. Mike breathes passionate pursuit of God, His nature, and His ways.

Then my endearing family and I moved to the wonderful Southern city called Nashville, Tennessee. There the shadow of a true father in the faith touched my life in none other than Don Finto. Papa Don is known for many things, but everyone will agree that he embodies a contagious love for God and His Word. These men and others have modeled for me the message contained in the radical read.

People often ask me how I do what I do. Well, when you surround yourself with a great team, it helps! With that in mind, I wish to recognize the loyal staff of Encounters Network and our intercessors around the globe who pray for me on an ongoing basis. Great gratitude also goes to my writing assistant, Kathy Deering, in this and many other projects. What a delight it has been to partner with Bob Whitaker Jr., Don Milam, and the amazing team at Whitaker House. This is my first work with this publishing house—but it won't be my last.

I want to see true disciples of Jesus arise across the face of the earth whose chief aim in life is "to worship God and enjoy Him forever"! With a heart of gratitude, I have chosen to dedicate this book to the Lover of my soul, my Best Friend and constant companion: the glorious Lord Jesus Christ Himself. To Him belong the honor, the glory, and the dominion, both now and forevermore!

With a love for God and His amazing ways,
James W. Goll

Foreword

Passionate Pursuit: Getting to Know God and His Word illuminates an essential truth for us as individual believers and for the body of Christ as a whole. It is an element I have preached about for many years: We must emphasize the Word *and* the Spirit as we deepen our relationship with God and expand our role as ambassadors for Christ in the world. The need of the hour is not one or the other—Word or Spirit—but both!

As James Goll writes, "The Father, Son, and Holy Spirit want you to become intimately familiar with the Word because, by doing so, you will get to know the One who inspired every line." He also says, "If you want to know God's heart, then you must know His Word, where His nature and character are revealed."

To know God personally is to experience the reality and power of our faith. James Goll affirms that the more we learn about God through His Word, the better we will understand Him and come to know Him in a profound way. And, the more we know Him, the more clearly we will reflect His image, and the better we will be able to fulfill what He calls us to do by His Spirit—even that which initially seems "impossible" to our human imagination.

I encourage you to allow the depth of the Word and the fellowship of the Spirit to fill your heart and mind as you passionately pursue almighty God—the One who is our Creator, Redeemer, and loving Father.

—*R. T. Kendall*
Author of 60 books
Former Senior Minister, Westminster Chapel, London

Section One

To Know Him Is to Love Him

Augustine described theology as the reasoning or discussion concerning the Deity. In this first section of *Passionate Pursuit*, I seek to transcend the traditional conversation on theology. Chapters 1–7 do not deal with the "rational" approach to God, His Son, and the Holy Spirit. They are a manifesto of my views about God based upon biblical truth and personal experience. Therefore, this first section is about knowing God personally.

In chapter 1, I lay the foundation by referring to a quote by Blaise Pascal from his book *Pensées*. Pascal said that every person has within him an "infinite abyss" (a concept some have described as a "God-shaped vacuum"), and that this abyss "can only be filled by an infinite and immutable object, that is to say, only by God Himself."[1]

This vacuum creates a great hunger within us until we arrive at the place where we see God as a personal Father. On that journey of passionate pursuit, we make wonderful discoveries that unveil the marvelous names and attributes of our loving God as manifested in Father, Son, and Holy Spirit—the Three in One. These are the themes of chapters 2 and 3.

---

1. Blaise Pascal, *Pascal's Pensées* (New York: E. P. Dutton & Co., Inc., 1958), Section VII, "Morality and Doctrine," 113, http://www.gutenberg.org/files/18269/18269-h/18269-h.htm.

Chapter 4 presents one of the most famous questions ever asked. Like a master psychologist probing for the truth, Jesus asked His disciples, *"Who do you say that I am?"* (See, for example, Matthew 16:15.) How you answer that question will reveal the depth of your understanding of God as revealed through His Son. So, in chapters 4 and 5, I offer you the answer to that question as unveiled in the birth, life, suffering, death, burial, and resurrection of Jesus Christ the Messiah. The prophet Isaiah wrote, *"You are a God who hides Himself"* (Isaiah 45:15). Jesus unveils the mysterious God and puts a face on that hidden reality. In Christ, we see God in all His beauty.

Then, in chapters 6 and 7, we come to what theology calls "the third Person of the Trinity," the Person of the Holy Spirit. He is the "executive power" behind the scenes who has come to execute the will of God through His servants by empowering and gifting them to perform that will. He is the "alongside One" who makes the grace and glory of God a reality in the affairs of men and women as He connects heaven with earth.

1

God as Our Personal Father

Man's chief end is to glorify God, and to enjoy him forever.
—Westminster Shorter Catechism

It has been stated that man was created with an internal void that only God Himself can fill. I, for one, believe this to be so. Every single person is on a constant search to find fulfillment in this life—meaning, purpose, and destiny. We were created this way. You and I were fashioned in such a manner.

Did you know that the depth of your hunger is the length of your reach to God? In fact, you can be as close to God as you want to be. After all, God is an "equal opportunity employer." Draw near to Him, and He will draw near to you. (See James 4:8.) I have made statements like these to believers all around the world. They provoke people spiritually and make them desire more of God, causing them to search for Him. We are to be in passionate pursuit after God Himself. Right?

Actually, when I first heard some of these declarations, they disturbed me. Like bits of sand in an oyster, such principles initially irritated me because they sounded like clichés. They seemed self-righteous, pompous, hyper-spiritual—and unobtainable. But, as they have worked for years within my heart and my inner being, I trust that the irritants are being shaped into a pearl of great price.

I kept thinking, *Well, I do want to be close to God! I do want to know His heart!* I had to look deeper within, persistently.... I went on many walks. I went on many talks. Eventually, I decided on what I wanted more than anything. More than being a great leader of a nation, the greatest orator, a profound innovator, or the most highly gifted evangelist—even more than being a renowned singer or a legendary missionary (which are all great pursuits, by the way)—I wanted to *know God!*

I have since been on a journey that the world often scoffs at. By grace, I made an internal decision to follow a path less traveled in our fast-paced society—to take time to get to know my Creator intimately, so that I could enjoy Him forever. That became the chief aim of my life.

Will you join me in this type of passionate pursuit of God?

Getting to Know Father

"Our Father..." (Matthew 6:9). That simple pair of words is one of the greatest and most complete revelations about God.

God is a Father—a Father who wants a family. He yearns for a family. Jesus is His only begotten Son (see, for example, John 1:14), but He is not an only child. His Father has many children, and Jesus has many brothers and sisters. The apostle Paul recognized the family nature of our relationship with God when he wrote, *"I bow my knees before the Father, from whom every family in heaven and on earth derives its name"* (Ephesians 3:14–15). God's big heavenly family does not include any "grandchildren," by the way, since our Father accepts only first-generation children. He is our Father in two respects: first, because He created us, and second, because we have said yes to His invitation to be reborn as full sons and daughters of His kingdom.

God is our Father because He created us and because we accepted His invitation to be reborn as His sons and daughters.

Sometimes, we unknowingly limit God's fatherhood in our lives. We think He is Father God only to certain special people, so we do not approach Him in that way. But He is not Father only of (for example) the first humans He created, Adam and Eve. Nor is He Father only of the holiest men and women who have worshipped Him over the centuries. He is not Father solely of Isaiah and Micah and Malachi and Deborah and Barak; of Ruth and Naomi; of Esther and Ezra and Nehemiah; of Daniel and Shadrach, Meshach, and Abednego. He did not elevate to "son status" only the twelve disciples of Jesus, along with Jesus' closest friends, Mary, Martha, and Lazarus. After He died, Jesus did not summon only the apostle Paul into His Father's family. He does not give preference to spiritual giants. You don't have to be a John Wesley or a George Müller or a D. L. Moody or a Billy Graham or a Mother Teresa or a Reinhard Bonnke to address Him as Father.

To call Him Father, you don't have to be a spiritual giant at all.

The truth is that each and every one of us can call Him Father, every day of our lives. Anybody who has been "born again"—who has received the completed work of God's Son Jesus (His crucifixion, burial, resurrection from the dead, and ascension) and who has accepted His invitation to follow—is included in His family.

We are God's sons and daughters. He is our Father. How wonderfully simple, and yet how amazingly profound!

The Father's Blessing

None of us can claim to be self-sufficient, just as none of us who is an earthly father can claim to be a perfect father. We need our heavenly Father. Every single individual who has ever lived has been created in the image of God (see Genesis 1:26–27), but unless we walk with Him, we will never realize what that means.

We were created to *need* the Father. Without the Father's love and the Father's blessing, we are sunk. We may seek love and blessing in a variety of places, but unless those places point us to Father God, they will ultimately hold us back. No counselor or other expert can take the Father's place; no mentor or husband or wife—not even a great father figure—can meet our real need for love and blessing. Every one of these people is just as human as we are.

Yet God uses human vessels to represent Him and to point to Him. In the Old Testament, we read about the powerful effect that a patriarchal father's blessing could have. (Read, for example, chapters 27 and 49 of the book of Genesis.) Once these blessings were given, they could never be revoked, even by the father who had bestowed them (and even if he had been tricked into blessing the wrong son, as happened with Isaac and his twin sons, Esau and Jacob).

Since our earthly models of fatherhood are inadequate, how can we ever hope to receive the fullness of our heavenly Father's love? We must lean hard on the fact that God's love—which has sought us out individually—*will* be able to reach our hearts, even through imperfect vessels. As we seek God's face, He will bring people into our lives who will impart His love to us. That includes spiritual pioneers who have gone before us, who have left us writings and "footprints" to follow. As we honor these fellow "cracked pots," we can drink deeply from their wells of God's love. Receiving His love and acceptance restores our damaged spirits and souls.

Redemptive Gleaning

An aspect of God's redemption is that He allows us to glimpse His shadow through other members of His adopted family. I call this "redemptive gleaning." In my own life, I have had to glean in this way. My own natural father had many limitations. As I was growing up, I was afraid of him most of the time, and yet I honored him and cared deeply for him. Still, I could never quite call him "Father," because I couldn't really connect with him in that manner. We were very different from one other, and, honestly, he did not come across as if he understood me very well.

However, toward the end of my father's journey here on earth, the Holy Spirit convinced me, through a series of dreams and visions, that I needed to go back home to receive my "father's blessing." I was uncertain, and—because of our on and off dysfunctional family history, and his current debilitating diabetic situation—I was more than cautious. Yet God convinced me of my need, and He even went out of His way to make it possible.

My dad had authentically come to faith later in life, and I eventually even had the honor of leading him in water baptism. However, like many other believers, he still had a lot of emotional wounds and some leftover baggage. But then—God! In my dad's hour of weakness, God gave him a couple of supernatural dreams, and he knew that he had a son who could interpret them, so he asked me if he could talk with me, one-on-one.

So we had that one-on-one talk. We discussed his upbringing, how he had grown up during the Depression as the oldest of seven children in a family with a German background. He'd had to work extremely hard, and he'd been kicked out of the house when he was twelve years old to raise himself. He'd never known the love of a father. I could tell you more, but I don't really need to. It was clear that he never could have given away something he himself had not received.

The conversation shifted, and he started off with, "Son…."

I was forty-four years old at the time, and I could not remember ever before hearing him call me "Son." Something like a supernatural current of love started flowing from his heart to mine and back, maybe something that had been pent up for years. With a tear coming down his big cheek, he said, "Son, I never understood you all your life. How did you get so close to God?"

After I collected myself, I answered, "Father, as far as I know…." And that was the first time in my memory that I had ever, from my heart, called him "Father." I told him how my mother, his wife, had dedicated me to Christ's service before I was ever conceived, a fact that he knew about and confirmed. The atmosphere was pregnant with the love and comfort of God. We joined hands. He did not pray out loud, but I know he prayed. I prayed out loud, and I blessed him. That day, I called him "Father," and he called me "Son." Not long after that, he graduated to heaven. And yes, I was honored to speak at my *father's* funeral.

A Confirmation Is Released

To tie it up perfectly, I had a wonderful experience a few months later while I was ministering in Atlanta, Georgia. At the close of my session on "Gatekeepers of His Presence," I saw a vision of my father's face in which he was healed and in robust health. His rosy cheeks were back, and his blue eyes were gleaming. And I heard these words in my heart from the Holy Spirit: *I have a word to give you from your father.*

Just at that moment, a Canadian man who was also ministering laid his hands on me and prophesied, "There have been those in your life who have never understood you, but God has used all of this to create a brokenness in you so that the fragrance of Christ will be released through your life that will go across the earth."

When he lifted his hands off me and remained in a posture of worship unto the Lord, I saw my father's face in a vision beaming at me a second time. I then heard these words, which have forever changed my life: *I understand you now.* I sobbed under the goodness of God and the healing grace of Jesus Christ.

Do you see how God uses imperfect vessels to transmit His love to us? Imperfect vessels are all He has to use, and His perfect love comes through every time.

Receive the Father's Love

You have to be intentional about receiving the Father's love. Seek God. Be passionate about it. Open your heart and accept the free gift of the Father's love through Jesus Christ His Son. You can receive the love of God in multiple ways, such as the following:

+ a relationship with the Word of God

+ soaking in the Holy Spirit's presence

+ reading about the lessons of church history and about leaders who have known the depths of His love

+ redemptively gleaning glimpses of His shadow through your earthly family members

+ honoring the anointing of the Holy Spirit upon veterans of the faith

Drink deeply! Receive the blessing and love of God. When the prophet Elijah was taken into heaven in a chariot, his disciple Elisha saw the chariot carry him upward, and he cried out, "*My father, my father...!*" (2 Kings 2:12). Elisha looked around and found that Elijah's mantle of prophetic blessing had been left behind for him, and he took it up. (See 2 Kings

2:9–14.) As a result, he was able to walk for the rest of his life in a double portion of the power of the Holy Spirit, with great confidence. Perhaps Elisha saw into a revelation of fatherhood. He saw Elijah as his father and mentor, but then he received the greater revelation: he saw the Father of Elijah—God Himself!

You have to be intentional about receiving the Father's love. Seek God. Be passionate about it.

No two people have the same experience of the Father's love, because every child of God is unique. In words that ended up being the last verse of the Old Testament, the prophet Malachi promised a last-day move of God in which the Holy Spirit would *"restore the hearts of the fathers to their children and the hearts of the children to their fathers, so that [God would] not come and smite the land with a curse"* (Malachi 4:6). In our pilgrimage of becoming all that God has called us to be, may each of us experience the security that comes with knowing Him as our personal Father. May each one of us be able to enter into the Father's blessing! May each of us grow in our earnest longing to know God's heart and to reveal it to others.

So, let us continue now in our journey of discovering the heart of God and His Word!

2

The Unfolding Revelation of God

The yearning to know What cannot be known,
to comprehend the Incomprehensible,
to touch and taste the Unapproachable,
arises from the image of God in the nature of man.
Deep calleth unto deep, and though polluted and landlocked by
the mighty disaster theologians call the Fall,
the soul senses its origin and longs to return to its Source.[2]
—A. W. Tozer

I love learning about the Father. I love reviewing the ABCs about Him. I revel in the way He is always revealing more about Himself, continually unwrapping gifts of revelation. The progressive unfolding of discovery about God shouldn't amaze me, but it does. It just keeps taking me by surprise, and it delights me. The more I yearn for Him, the more He reveals another side of His nature to me. The same can be true for you, as well.

This heavenly Father is someone who can be encountered. You may not be able to see Him with your eyes, but you can encounter His presence. You can know His heart!

---

2. A. W. Tozer, *The Knowledge of the Holy* (New York: HarperCollins Publishers, 1961), 9.

Another way of stating it is this: God is always present tense. He is not only the God of history; He is the God of "now." He is the I Am, as Moses found out when he encountered Him:

> Then Moses said to God, "Behold, I am going to the sons of Israel, and I will say to them, 'The God of your fathers has sent me to you.' Now they may say to me, 'What is His name?' What shall I say to them?" God said to Moses, "I Am Who I Am"; and He said, "Thus you shall say to the sons of Israel, 'I Am has sent me to you.'"
>
> (Exodus 3:13–14)

God said, "*I Am Who I Am.*" He didn't say, "I am the God who 'was,'" or "I am the God who 'will be.'" One of the greatest revelations about Him is that He always *is*. That means He is always available, and He can always be encountered. He always hears you. You can always run to Him. He is not far away—He is always near!

Here's a fresh take on the last sentence of the above Scripture passage: "I Am has sent Myself to you," or "I send Me to you." God was dispatching Moses to lead the children of Israel, but He was also sending Himself. Moses would be His ambassador, or spokesman, and God would have a living, vibrant relationship with him. Moses modeled this relationship for Israel; and, consequently, he modeled it for us.

Here is the God who created the universe, and yet He is relational. He already knows you inside and out, and He wants you to know Him. He wants us all to know His heart.

God is not far away—He is always near!

A God of Many Names

The more I know God, the more I want to know more about Him. God goes by many names besides I Am. Each name reveals to us a different aspect of His nature, because His names help us to encounter and to perceive His various characteristics. The names below are only some of the ones by which He is best known. Even taken together, these names give us merely a glimpse of God's attributes; they make up only a tiny portion of who He really is.

Jehovah Jireh (**The Lord Will Provide**). When God provided a ram for Abraham's sacrifice as a substitute for his son, Isaac, He identified Himself as the God who provides. *"Abraham called the name of that place The Lord Will Provide, as it is said to this day, 'In the mount of the Lord it will be provided'"* (Genesis 22:14).

Jehovah Nissi (**The Lord Is My Banner**). Over and over in the Bible, God revealed Himself through special circumstances. After Joshua prevailed decisively against the enemies of Israel (the Israelites kept winning as long as Moses kept holding his hands up), *"Moses built an altar and named it The Lord is My Banner"* (Exodus 17:15). The Lord is our champion and defender, protecting us from all the power of the evil one.

Jehovah Shalom (**The Lord Is Peace**). Gideon, who later became a warrior and judge in Israel, was dismayed when he realized that the angel of the Lord had visited him. But God reassured him.

> *When Gideon saw that he was the angel of the Lord, he said, "Alas, O Lord God! For now I have seen the angel of the Lord face to face." The Lord said to him, "Peace to you, do not fear; you shall not die." Then Gideon built an altar there to the Lord and named it The Lord is Peace.* (Judges 6:22–24)

Jehovah Tsidkenu (**The Lord Our Righteousness**). God does not say only that He Himself is righteous but that He puts us in right standing, too.

> *And this is His name by which He will be called, "The Lord our righteousness."...In those days Judah will be saved and Jerusalem will dwell in safety; and this is the name by which she will be called: the Lord is our righteousness.* (Jeremiah 23:6; 33:16)

Jehovah Rapha (**The Lord Our Healer**). The people of Israel, weary and thirsty, despaired when they arrived at some much-needed water in the desert, only to discover that it was bitter and undrinkable. Then

Moses performed a prophetic act that prefigured the way Jesus' cross transforms our bitterness into sweetness, and he spoke the words of the miracle-working Lord:

> *If you will give earnest heed to the voice of the* Lord *your God, and do what is right in His sight, and give ear to His commandments, and keep all His statutes, I will put none of the diseases on you which I have put on the Egyptians; for I, the* Lord, *am your healer.*
>
> (Exodus 15:26)

Jehovah Shammah (The Lord Is Present). Strictly speaking, this is one of the new names for Jerusalem, and yet the term identifies the city closely with the Person of the Prince of Peace, the Messiah. (See Isaiah 9:6.) Jerusalem is being personified according to the characteristics of the Lord God, who will be present there: "*The name of the city from that day shall be, 'The* Lord *is there'*" (Ezekiel 48:35).

Jehovah Rophe (The Lord Is Our Shepherd). As has been portrayed so often in pictorial illustrations, sermons, poetry, and hymn lyrics, God is our Shepherd. In the words of the familiar psalm, "*The* Lord *is my shepherd, I shall not want*" (Psalm 23:1).

Holy One of Israel. The following verse is only one of the many places in Scripture where God is referred to as the Holy One of Israel: "*I will also praise You with a harp, even Your truth, O my God; to You I will sing praises with the lyre, O Holy One of Israel*" (Psalm 71:22).

The Judge. Whether we like it or not, God *is* the ultimate Judge, because the Creator has full authority over what He has created, whether it's still alive on earth, or dead and buried. "*Shall not the Judge of all the earth deal justly?*" (Genesis 18:25).

Eternal God. This name may seem obvious, but "eternal" describes one of God's most important attributes—He has no beginning or end, and He does not change. "*The eternal God is your refuge, and underneath are the everlasting arms*" (Deuteronomy 33:27 niv).

Almighty. We use this name more often than some of the others, referring to God as "God Almighty," or sometimes simply as "the Almighty."

"*The* LORD *appeared to Abram and said to him, 'I am Almighty God; walk before Me and be blameless'*" (Genesis 17:1 NKJV).

Fortress. God is a strong tower for all who run to Him. (See Proverbs 18:10.) He will shelter and protect us. David said,

> *The Lord is my Rock [of escape from Saul] and my Fortress [in the wilderness] and my Deliverer; my God, my Rock, in Him will I take refuge; my Shield and the Horn of my salvation; my Stronghold and my Refuge, my Savior—You save me from violence.*
>
> (2 Samuel 22:2–3 AMP)

The LORD. Jews have used the Hebrew equivalent of this name of God with fear and trembling, declining even to utter it aloud and thus rendering it without vowels as the tetragrammaton YHWH, which we pronounce "Yahweh" or "Jehovah." "*I appeared to Abraham, Isaac, and Jacob, as God Almighty, but by My name,* LORD *[YHWH], I did not make Myself known to them*" (Exodus 6:3).

Living God. So that we won't miss this aspect of His nature, God reveals Himself as the living God, a fierce warrior who reigns supreme over everything, living or dead. "*The living God is among you*" (Joshua 3:10).

Lord of Hosts. What are "hosts"? They are armies or multitudes. And what does it mean to be the "Lord of Hosts"? It means that God is the Commander in Chief of all the hosts of heaven—the mighty, unseen army of heavenly beings. "[Hannah, future mother of Samuel the prophet] *made a vow and said, 'O* LORD *of hosts...'*" (1 Samuel 1:11). In the *New International Version*, "LORD *of hosts*" is translated "LORD *Almighty.*"

Lord of Sabaoth. This name is not related to the word *Sabbath*, although the term looks almost the same to us. It is another way of saying "LORD of Hosts," and it is found only in the New Testament. One instance is in Romans 9:29, and the other is in the book of James: "*Behold, the pay of the laborers who mowed your fields, and which has been withheld by you, cries out against you; and the outcry of those who did the harvesting has reached the ears of the Lord of Sabaoth*" (James 5:4).

Lord of Lords. God is also the Commander in Chief over all others who hold positions of authority. "*For the* LORD *your God is God of gods and*

Lord of lords, the great God, mighty and awesome, who shows no partiality and accepts no bribes" (Deuteronomy 10:17 NIV).

Our Strength. Immediately after God demonstrated His power by dividing the Red Sea in half so that the people of Israel could escape from their Egyptian captors, Moses led the people in a song that began like this:

> *The LORD is my strength and song, and He has become my salvation; this is my God, and I will praise Him; my father's God, and I will extol Him.* (Exodus 15:2)

Most High. God is known as the Most High throughout the Bible—in the Old Testament and the New Testament alike. Here is one example:

> *When the Most High gave the nations their inheritance, when He separated the sons of man, He set the boundaries of the peoples according-ing to the number of the sons of Israel.* (Deuteronomy 32:8)

Father of Lights. James reveals another of God's names, along with the attribute of God that the name portrays: *"Every good thing given and every perfect gift is from above, coming down from the Father of lights, with whom there is no variation or shifting shadow"* (James 1:17).

The Greatest Revelation of All

We would not have the capacity to worship this God who is Almighty, Most High, Eternal, Lord of Hosts, and much more if it weren't for the attributes reflected in His best name of all: *Father.* This God opens His heart wide and says, "Children!" Thus, this intimidating God is also approachable. His Son Jesus said so: *"All things have been handed over to Me by My Father; and no one knows the Son except the Father; nor does anyone know the Father except the Son, **and anyone to whom the Son wills to reveal Him"*** (Matthew 11:27).

Jesus' messenger Paul wrote to the church in Corinth, *"Grace to you and peace from God our Father and the Lord Jesus Christ"* (2 Corinthians 1:2). He didn't say, "Grace to you and peace from the Almighty," or "...from God Our Deliverer," or "...from God Most High," but rather "...*from God* our Father." Again, Paul shed a little more light on the idea when he wrote a letter to the church in Ephesus, saying, *"For this reason I bow my knees before the Father, from whom every family in heaven and on earth derives its name…"* (Ephesians 3:14–15).

As I said at the beginning of this chapter, God wants a family. He desperately wants sons and daughters to relate to. He craves fellowship. Over the centuries, He has made it abundantly clear that He is first and foremost *our Father.* Who wouldn't want to know a God like that?

We would not have the capacity to worship almighty God except for His fatherhood.

God Is Called "Father" Throughout the Bible

In both the Old Testament (the "old covenant") and the New Testament (the "new covenant"), you can easily find references to God as Father. The following is a "Father God sampler."

From the Old Covenant

If you read through Genesis and the rest of the Pentateuch (the first five books of the Bible, also known as the Five Books of Moses), you will discover that most of the "father" references have to do with earthly fathers. Yet in the fifth book, you will come to these lines: *"Do you thus repay the LORD, O foolish and unwise people? Is not He your Father who has bought you? He has made you and established you"* (Deuteronomy 32:6).

As you continue to read through the Old Testament and come to the book of Psalms, you will start to see a few more indications that God is our Father. Here are two examples:

> *A father to the fatherless, a defender of widows, is God in his holy dwelling. God sets the lonely in families….*   (Psalm 68:5–6 NIV)

> *Just as a father has compassion on his children, so the LORD has compassion on those who fear Him.*   (Psalm 103:13)

In such psalms, God is revealing Himself not only as a Father but also as a *compassionate* Father. A compassionate father is approachable; God the Father invites His children to come near Him.

Moving on, you will come to the book of the prophet Isaiah. While we usually think of the following verse as messianic prophecy, descriptive of Jesus, look at the exact wording that is included (*"Eternal* **Father***"*):

> For a child will be born to us, a son will be given to us; and the govern-ment will rest on His shoulders; and His name will be called Wonder-ful Counselor, Mighty God, Eternal Father, Prince of Peace.
>
> (Isaiah 9:6)

And, the prophet tells us, just as a potter forms the clay as he wishes, so the Father forms us; we are the works of His hands:

> But now, O LORD, You are our Father, we are the clay, and You our potter; and all of us are the work of Your hand.   (Isaiah 64:8)

Toward the end of the Old Testament, we find these lines in the book of Malachi: *"Have we not all one Father? Has not one God created us?"* (Malachi 2:10 NKJV).

From the New Covenant

As you might expect, due to the revelation of God through Jesus, we find a much greater abundance of references to God as Father when we open the New Testament. Jesus, the Son of God—sent by His Father to dwell in human form in the midst of the nation of Israel—revealed God as Father throughout His ministry. We know that even before He began to teach His band of disciples, He mentioned God as Father at least once—when He was only twelve years old and had stayed behind in Jerusalem at Passover without telling His parents.

> When [Jesus' parents] *did not find him, they went back to Jerusalem to look for him. After three days they found him in the temple courts, sitting among the teachers, listening to them and asking them questions. Everyone who heard him was amazed at his understanding and his answers. When his parents saw him, they were astonished. His mother*

*said to him, "Son, why have you treated us like this? Your father and I
have been anxiously searching for you." "Why were you searching for
me?" he asked. "Didn't you know I had to be in my Father's house?"
But they did not understand what he was saying to them.*

(Luke 2:45–50 NIV)

The New Testament centers on the revelation of the Son—and where
there is a Son, there must be a Father! In His teaching and preaching, Jesus
cited examples and told stories about fathers and sons in order to underline
what He was saying. He compared God the Father to earthly fathers, in
terms of His desire to bless His children: *"If you then, being evil, know how
to give good gifts to your children, how much more will your Father who is in
heaven give what is good to those who ask Him!"* (Matthew 7:11).

Jesus cautioned against giving too much honor to an earthly leader,
compared with the honor that is due to the Father of all: *"Do not call anyone
on earth 'father,' for you have one Father, and he is in heaven"* (Matthew 23:9
NIV).

Most memorably, when the disciples asked Jesus to teach them to pray,
He started by explaining to them how to address God. He didn't start out
with "O Buddha…" or "O great Creator and Architect of the Universe…"
but rather *"Our Father in heaven…"* (Luke 11:2 NKJV).

Why does He want us to start off that way? Because we're in a relationship with God. You and I and anyone else in Christ who prays to God are
all children of the Father. You could even say that the Father is inviting us
to come up and sit in His lap and talk to Him.

We need to remember where Jesus came from. John said it best: *"And
the Word became flesh and dwelt among us, and we beheld His glory, the glory
as of the only begotten of the Father, full of grace and truth"* (John 1:14 NKJV).
Jesus came from someplace (heaven). And He came from Someone (the
Father). He represents the finest expression of the Father's heart. Out of
the Father's heart of love, of nourishment, of rest, and of safety issued the
Son, who is the very heart of His Father. Lest we lose track of the fact that
God and the Father are one and the same, Paul repeated the concept "one
God and Father" in a variety of ways, such as in the following passages:

For even if there are so-called gods whether in heaven or on earth, as
indeed there are many gods and many lords, yet for us there is but one
God, the Father....   (1 Corinthians 8:5–6)

...one God and Father of all who is over all and through all and in
all.   (Ephesians 4:6)

...every tongue will confess that Jesus Christ is Lord, to the glory of
God the Father.   (Philippians 2:11)

From a fascinating line in the book of Hebrews, we learn that God
is the "Father of spirits": *"We had earthly fathers to discipline us, and we*
respected them; shall we not much rather be subject to the Father of spirits, and
live?" (Hebrews 12:9). We humans are spirit beings who will never die, and
we know that each human son or daughter has a spirit. And God takes care
of each of our spirits personally, like a loving human father personally cares
for and disciplines his children.

The apostle Peter wrote about how we should conduct ourselves as
children under our heavenly Father's oversight:

And if you call upon Him as [your] Father Who judges each one im-
partially according to what he does, [then] you should conduct your-
selves with true reverence throughout the time of your temporary resi-
dence [on the earth, whether long or short].   (1 Peter 1:17 AMP)

John expanded on our role, explaining that we are meant to minister to
our Father with our worship and our reverential conduct: "[Jesus] *has made*
us kings and priests to His God and Father, to Him be glory and dominion
forever and ever" (Revelation 1:6 NKJV).

Again, this is just a brief sampling of the many passages of Scripture
that refer to God as Father. In effect, I intentionally "skipped a stone"
across the Old and New Testaments, choosing verses to represent various
parts of the Bible. Christianity is different from other forms of religion,
and one significant reason is that we worship and serve a God whom we
address as "Father."

Yes, God is Captain of the Armies of Heaven, and much more, but He is also our "Papa," and He wants us to live with Him forever.

Jesus' Purpose for Coming to Earth

We would have only the vaguest idea about God being our Father if He had not sent His Son Jesus to make that fact obvious. Actually, the whole purpose of Jesus' coming to earth was to make known God's fatherhood and to reveal Himself as the way to God the Father. This is exactly what He told His disciples.

> *Jesus answered, "I am the way and the truth and the life. No one comes to the Father except through me. If you really know me, you will know my Father as well. From now on, you do know him and have seen him." Philip said, "Lord, show us the Father and that will be enough for us." Jesus answered: "Don't you know me, Philip, even after I have been among you such a long time? Anyone who has seen me has seen the Father. How can you say, 'Show us the Father'?"* (John 14:6–9 NIV)

Jesus is the exact representation of the Father. (See Hebrews 1:3.) Anyone who wants to get to know the Father can do so by passionately pursuing Him via a relationship with His Son, because the Son is just like His Father. Even though Jesus is just like God (and *is* God), He considers the Father to be more important than He is. He said to His disciples, *"If you loved Me, you would rejoice because I said, 'I am going to the Father,' for My Father is greater than I"* (John 14:28 NKJV).

Jesus' purpose for coming to earth was to make known God's fatherhood and to reveal Himself as the way to the Father.

Jesus came to prepare a place for us in the Father's house. Just as He came from the bosom of the Father (see John 1:18), so He returned to the Father (see John 20:17), and now He invites us to come with Him to dwell together with the Father. What is this place that Jesus prepares for us? It is the same place that He returned to, a place right in the middle of the Father's heart. God's heart is our destination. Yes, that's what Jesus said:

> *In My Father's house are many dwelling places; if it were not so, I would have told you; for I go to prepare a place for you. If I go and prepare a place for you, I will come again and receive you to Myself, that where I am, there you may be also.*   (John 14:2–3)

Jesus came from a place of glory, and He returned to that heavenly realm. He desperately wants to bring us there with Him. He has such a deep desire to bring us to Himself—it is so deep that He was willing to suffer and die for us. Look at the depth of relationship, the passion and the yearning, portrayed in Jesus' words to His Father regarding us:

> *I glorified You on the earth, having accomplished the work which You have given Me to do. Now, Father, glorify Me together with Your-self, with the glory which I had with You before the world was. I have manifested Your name to the men whom You gave Me out of the world; they were Yours and You gave them to Me, and they have kept Your word....Father, I desire that they also, whom You have given Me, be with Me where I am, so that they may see My glory which You have given Me, for You loved Me before the foundation of the world. O righteous Father, although the world has not known You, yet I have known You; and these have known that You sent Me; and I have made Your name known to them, and will make it known, so that the love with which You loved Me may be in them, and I in them.*
>
> (John 17:4–6, 24–26)

Without a doubt, Jesus came so that we could partake of the Father's love, both here on earth and forever in His glorious heaven. That love becomes "three-dimensional" to us when we read about it in John's writings. No other writer in the entire sixty-six books of the Bible told us more about the Father's love than John did. In addition to his gospel, he wrote three letters (1, 2, and 3 John) and the book of Revelation.

I used to wonder how John could be so explicit about what Jesus said regarding God the Father, and then I remembered that John was the disciple who had laid his head on Jesus' chest at the Last Supper. Since Jesus is the exact representation of His Father, that means that John heard the pulsating rhythm of God's heart. He heard the very heartbeat of the Father! Oh, I ache for such a thing! And John passed along to us what he "heard," using the simple language that a father might use with his children.

> Beloved, let us love one another, for love is from God; and everyone who loves is born of God and knows God. The one who does not love does not know God, for God is love. By this the love of God was manifested in us, that God has sent His only begotten Son into the world so that we might live through Him. In this is love, not that we loved God, but that He loved us and sent His Son to be the propitiation for our sins. Beloved, if God so loved us, we also ought to love one another. No one has seen God at any time; if we love one another, God abides in us, and His love is perfected in us. By this we know that we abide in Him and He in us, because He has given us of His Spirit. We have seen and testify that the Father has sent the Son to be the Savior of the world.
>
> (1 John 4:7–14)

The Holy Spirit's Purpose for Coming to Us

Revealing the Son and the Father

The following message is just as true now as it was twenty-one hundred years ago, and the Holy Spirit bears witness in our hearts that it is true today and every day. According to Jesus, the reason He sent the Spirit to dwell within our hearts is this:

> When he, the Spirit of truth, comes, he will guide you into all the truth. He will not speak on his own; he will speak only what he hears, and he will tell you what is yet to come. He will glorify me because it is from me that he will receive what he will make known to you. All that belongs to the Father is mine. That is why I said the Spirit will receive from me what he will make known to you.　　(John 16:13–15 NIV)

The Holy Spirit's purpose in coming to Jesus' followers is to reveal the Son and the Father to those who have bent their heads in a direction that is different from that of the world, in order to have ears that hear. (See, for example, Matthew 11:7–15.) The Spirit does not speak about Himself; He points to Another. Jesus points to Another, as well. Everything points to the revelation of God as our Father!

The Spirit of Adoption

In fact, one of the biggest reasons God the Father sent His Spirit to us, through Jesus, was to complete the adoption process for His newly adopted sons and daughters. This is why the Holy Spirit is known as the Spirit of Adoption.

> *For all who are being led by the Spirit of God, these are sons of God. For you have not received a spirit of slavery leading to fear again, but you have received a spirit of adoption as sons by which we cry out, "Abba! Father!" The Spirit Himself testifies with our spirit that we are children of God, and if children, heirs also, heirs of God and fellow heirs with Christ....* (Romans 8:14–17)

The term *"Abba"* is like the word *Daddy*, a more intimate and familiar word than *Father*. Those who are led by the Spirit—who follow Him—are the ones who can be called *"sons of God."* Daddy answers the child's questions, and He protects and guides. After adoption, a son or daughter of God matures by following the leading of the Holy Spirit. Maturation is always a process. It does not occur all at once in the moment a person is reborn. But the indestructible seed has been planted.

A son or daughter of God matures by following the leading of the Holy Spirit.

As we follow the Spirit of God, we learn to recognize our need for our Father. Through the Spirit of Adoption, this awareness builds within us until we cry out for Him. Our cries show our conviction, and our conviction has been preceded by a revelation furnished by the Spirit Himself about the depth of our need, as well as the more-than-sufficient supply that comes from the Father's heart. "Abba! Daddy! Father!" we cry out, as the Holy Spirit testifies with our human spirits that we are truly children of God.

The Amazing Love of God

See what great love the Father has lavished on us, that we should be called children of God! And that is what we are! The reason the world does not know us is that it did not know him....This is how we know what love is: Jesus Christ laid down his life for us. And we ought to lay down our lives for our brothers and sisters.　　(1 John 3:1, 16 NIV)

The Father's love has been manifested to us through His Son Jesus and His Holy Spirit alike. This love is amazing because it is limitless, and it is bestowed so freely upon us, His undeserving children. Once He adopts us, nothing at all can separate us from His love, because it is so strong.

What then shall we say to these things? If God is for us, who is against us? He who did not spare His own Son, but delivered Him over for us all, how will He not also with Him freely give us all things?...For I am convinced that neither death, nor life, nor angels, nor principalities, nor things present, nor things to come, nor powers, nor height, nor depth, nor any other created thing, will be able to separate us from the love of God, which is in Christ Jesus our Lord.　　(Romans 8:31–32, 38–39)

God invites us into a holy triangle of love, just as Jesus prayed, "Oh, Father, give them the kind of love that I have for You and that You have for Me." (See John 17:26.) The Father, the Son, and the Spirit are one; and the Spirit, the water, and the blood bear witness in agreement about this fact: *"For there are three that bear witness in heaven: the Father, the Word, and the Holy Spirit; and these three are one. And there are three that bear witness on earth: the Spirit, the water, and the blood; and these three agree as one"* (1 John 5:7–8 NKJV).

The phrase "Spirit, water, and blood" has many levels of meaning, including the washing, or the cleansing properties, of the Word and of the blood of Jesus Christ, who calls Himself the Living Water. (See, for example, the story of Jesus' meeting with the Samaritan woman at the well in John 4:7–38.) The Father, the Son, and the Spirit are love personified. This is the Godhead.

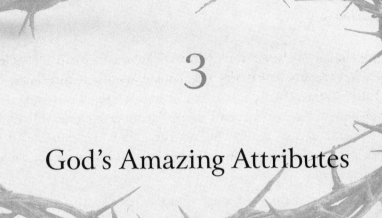

3

God's Amazing Attributes

…Wisdom…Infinitude…Sovereignty…Holiness…
Omniscience…Faithfulness…Love…
Omnipotence…Self-existence…Self-sufficiency…Justice…
Immutability…Mercy…Goodness…
Omnipresence…Immensity…Grace…Perfection…[3]

More, God!" has been the abandoned cry of the church, wave after wave, movement after movement. Although, sometimes, I'm not sure we are always prepared to have this prayer answered. Obviously, our human capacity is limited when we attempt (feebly) to describe God's divine characteristics, and when we consider receiving more of His presence. When I pause long enough to ponder His many amazing attributes, it just blows my mind—again. So, instead of wildly shouting, "More, God!" sometimes I can only quietly whisper, "God is More."

God is more than any theologian or scholar could comprehend in a lifetime, and He's more than the most passionate worshipper can sing and shout about. When I try to take another stab at describing His characteristics, I end up saying with the psalmist, *"Such knowledge is too wonderful for me; it is too high, I cannot attain to it"* (Psalm 139:6).

3. Attributes of God as listed by A. W. Tozer in the contents pages of his books *The Knowledge of the Holy* and *The Attributes of God*, volumes 1 and 2.

Our human limitations contribute to our misconceptions about God. For instance, because our energy is so limited, we may unconsciously assume that His energy must be, too. But it isn't. He is the *"Everlasting God"* (Isaiah 40:28). The Lord of the Universe does not get tired. He rested on the seventh day of Creation, but not because He was exhausted. (See Genesis 2:2–3.) No, when God unleashes His power, it does not deplete His supply at all.

This one fact should be enough to make "cessationists" think again. Has God's capacity for working miracles ceased? Was He more powerful two thousand years ago than He is today? Has He changed His mind about how He wants to demonstrate His power? I doubt it. (In fact, from my frame of reference, man's theological concept of cessationism is eventually going to cease, but God's almightiness will never cease.)

God alone is awesome. He is the *only* One to whom that word truly applies. We minimize the term *awesome* when we talk about "awesome weather," "awesome pizza," or even "awesome worship." Only God Himself is truly awesome.

> *Who is like You among the gods, O* Lord? *Who is like You, majestic in holiness, awesome in praises, working wonders?*   (Exodus 15:11)

Creation Points to the Creator

Our awesome God is the One who created the world, along with everything in it and on it, including you and me. That's why Paul wrote to the Christians in Rome to make sure they understood that even nonbelievers should be able to see God's handiwork and acknowledge His greatness:

> *For the wrath of God is revealed from heaven against all ungodliness and unrighteousness of men who suppress the truth in unrighteousness, because that which is known about God is evident within them; for God made it evident to them. For since the creation of the world His invisible attributes, His eternal power and divine nature, have been clearly seen, being understood through what has been made, so that they are without excuse.*   (Romans 1:18–20)

Does God exist? Nobody should wonder very long about that question if he or she looks around the created world. Both the reality of His existence and the fullness of His creativity and sovereignty should be obvious to all human beings, quite apart from any direct revelation by God through His spoken or written Word. Creation itself points to a divine Creator.

The Bible says that people who deny the existence of God should be considered—get this—"fools": *"The fool has said in his heart, 'There is no God.' They are corrupt, they have committed abominable deeds; there is no one who does good"* (Psalm 14:1). When we make statements such as "God has not left Himself without a witness," we're not necessarily talking about human witnesses but creation itself. For example, Paul and Barnabas said, *"Nevertheless He did not leave Himself without witness, in that He did good, gave us rain from heaven and fruitful seasons, filling our hearts with food and gladness"* (Acts 14:17 NKJV).

Creation points to its Author, the almighty God, and this fact cannot honestly be ignored or denied. The hills and valleys, the rivers and oceans, the profusion of plant and animal life, human beings in all their "wild and crazy" variety—the entire created world proves that one supreme God is behind it all. Nothing created itself.

Genesis 1:1 states, *"In the beginning God created the heavens and the earth."* In the beginning—before anything was here or there—God existed. He existed before anything else did. No one created Him. He has always been. (See, for example, Colossians 1:17.) God's preexistence places Him in a position of absolute supremacy: *"I am the Alpha and the Omega, the Beginning and the End, says the Lord God, He Who is and Who was and Who is to come, the Almighty (the Ruler of all)"* (Revelation 1:8 AMP). Everything that exists is a reality because God created it. The psalmist summed it up in this way:

> *Before the mountains were born or You gave birth to the earth and the world, even from everlasting to everlasting, You are God.*
> (Psalm 90:2)

There are many created beings in the universe, and they all bear the imprint of their Master. But there is only one Creator-God. Thus, the words that describe Him as supreme are ones that apply solely to Him. God is all-powerful (omnipotent); He is present everywhere at the same time (omnipresent); He is all-knowing (omniscient). He is amazing!

God's preexistence places Him in a position of absolute supremacy.

The Many Diverse Attributes of God

Since human beings were created in God's image, we ought to be able to figure out a few of God's attributes and qualities simply by extrapolating from what we know about ourselves. First, God created people to be spirit beings, like Himself. He also gave each of us a free will and a mind capable of reason. He gave us emotions and the ability to express them. Simply because we have these attributes, we can assume that God has these characteristics, too—in perfection. God is Spirit. God has free will. God is rational. God has emotions.

However, He is far above us, unmatched in power and knowledge. Nobody else, not even the archangels, even come close. (Satan, also called the devil, who is a fallen angel, is *not* all-powerful and all-knowing, even though people often seem to think he is.)

God's Omnipotence

Omnipotence is one of God's exclusive attributes. He shares it with no one. His acts and accomplishments could be performed only by an omnipotent being.

> *"To whom then will you liken Me, or to whom shall I be equal?" says the Holy One. Lift up your eyes on high, and see who has created these things, who brings out their host by number; He calls them all by name, by the greatness of His might and the strength of His power; not one is missing.* (Isaiah 40:25–26 NKJV)

Because God is omnipotent, we call him "Almighty." Absolutely nothing is beyond His ability. *"Ah Lord GOD! Behold, You have made the heavens and the earth by Your great power and by Your outstretched arm! Nothing is too difficult for You"* (Jeremiah 32:17). When God unleashes His power in an obvious way—for instance, by parting the Red Sea—He has no less power afterward than He did beforehand. His battery has not been drained in the least. He is all-powerful at all times and in all places.

He does not need to prove Himself. Being all-powerful does not tempt Him to do anything that would contradict His nature. Therefore, the all-powerful God does *not* use His power to do certain things. For instance, He does not lie. (See, for example, Titus 1:2; 2 Timothy 2:13.) He cannot sin, and He will not ignore sin. (See, for example, 1 John 3:9.) His power operates within the confines of His righteousness and love. His mighty actions are not governed by His power; His power is governed by His divine nature.

Bible teachers (and we preachers) talk a lot about the power of God. I think we should talk more about the God of Power. It makes the equation a lot more understandable.

God's Omnipresence

God is omnipresent, which means that He is present everywhere at the same time. This does not mean that God and the created world are one and the same; such a belief is called *pantheism*. Rather, God is separate and distinct from His creation. Yet He is dynamically present everywhere in His creation—which is to say, everywhere in the universe. Through the prophet Jeremiah, He said as much:

> "Am I only a God nearby," declares the LORD, "and not a God far away? Who can hide in secret places so that I cannot see them?" declares the LORD. "Do not I fill heaven and earth?" declares the LORD.
> (Jeremiah 23:23–24 NIV)

We find it easy to believe that God's presence fills heaven, because it is His "address," after all. Heaven is where He lives. But how could He *"fill"* the earth, with all its disorder and death? Some people think that God is too holy to abide alongside sin. Then again, others think that He stays away from us until He is invited to come, or that He will always be more reachable in certain special places. There is an element of truth in these concepts. But if you look in the Bible, which was written well after the fall of humankind, you will find plenty of evidence that He never stopped filling the whole sin-inflicted earth, whether or not at human bidding.

God did not lose the title deed to planet Earth due to the fall. Many people believe that the world belongs to the devil, but that idea is just not right. For the time being, the world system may be under the rule of the evil one, but the cosmos (the earth and then some) never stopped belonging to God. The old hymn says it quite well: "This is my Father's world"[4]!

Even Satan, that powerful fallen archangel, is not omnipresent. No angel (good or evil), and certainly no human being, can be present everywhere at the same time. The attribute of omnipresence is absolutely unique to God alone. Nothing escapes God's notice, not even the smallest sparrow (see, for example, Luke 12:6), because He is everywhere—under and over, inside and outside, behind and before, beside and between, near and far, around and throughout....

As King David noted in Psalm 139, no matter where he might go, the presence of God's Spirit would be there:

> *Where can I go from Your Spirit? Or where can I flee from Your presence? If I ascend to heaven, You are there; if I make my bed in Sheol, behold, You are there. If I take the wings of the dawn, if I dwell in the remotest part of the sea, even there Your hand will lead me, and Your right hand will lay hold of me. If I say, "Surely the darkness will overwhelm me, and the light around me will be night," even the darkness is not dark to You, and the night is as bright as the day. Darkness and light are alike to You.* (Psalm 139:7–12)

When David's son and successor, Solomon, dedicated the temple as the house of the Lord, he proclaimed that God's presence could not be confined to a building: *"But will God indeed dwell with mankind on the earth? Behold, heaven and the highest heaven cannot contain You; how much less this house which I have built"* (2 Chronicles 6:18). God is *Jehovah Shammah*, "the Lord Is Present"—He is ever present everywhere at every moment.

---

4. Maltbie D. Babcock, "This Is My Father's World," 1901.

No good deed goes unnoticed by God, and no sin goes unobserved by the all-present One. Acting like little children, some people seem to think that if they close the eyes of their hearts, they can hide from Him, because if they can't see Him, He can't see them. (See, for example, Psalm 94:7–9.) But, of course, He can see right through their attempts to conceal themselves; and, in this game of hide-and-seek, He seeks them out and finds them every time. More than that, He *loves* them. Nobody can get away from God's presence. He cannot be deterred from being present and available everywhere, from the highest snow-covered mountaintop to the blackest depths of the sea; from the magnificence of Buckingham Palace to the HIV-infected slums of Cité Soleil, Haiti. Our God is always present and always available. This is the kind of God I want to passionately pursue!

God's Omniscience

God's omnipresence points directly to another one of His divine attributes: omniscience. To be omniscient means to be "all-knowing." I love Isaiah's list of rhetorical questions about God:

> *Who has directed the Spirit of the* Lord, *or as His counselor has informed Him? With whom did He consult and who gave Him understanding? And who taught Him in the path of justice and taught Him knowledge and informed Him of the way of understanding?*
> (Isaiah 40:13–14)

Omniscience is intrinsic to God's nature; He has always known everything there is to know, and He always will. He sees and knows all that happened in the past, all that is and is not happening today, and all that will or will not occur in the future—without any props or reminders.

Our human knowledge comes from external sources, but God's knowledge is part of His nature. He did not need to read a how-to book before He created the earth. He just knew how. He did not have to study physiology in order to make Adam. He did not have to get a degree in astronomy to put the stars in their places. Likewise, Jesus the Son did not have to read a medical text before He healed people of their diseases and disabilities. He didn't have to read poems or sing romantic songs in order to learn to love. God *is* love. God *is* knowledge.

What makes people capable of creating and inventing things? God the Creator and Master Inventor has released a tiny portion of His divine creativity into their lives. They may think something is their own original idea, so that they hurry off to get a patent on it. But the knowledge about the idea belongs to God, as does the ultimate glory for its creation. Job found himself challenged by God in regard to a presumptuous attitude when the Lord said to him, *"Where were you when I laid the foundation of the earth? Tell Me, if you have understanding,....have you understood the expanse of the earth? Tell Me, if you know all this"* (Job 38:4, 18).

---

*Our human knowledge comes from external sources,
but God's knowledge is part of His nature.*

The psalmist was passionate about God's greatness: *"Great is our Lord and of great power; His understanding is inexhaustible and boundless"* (Psalm 147:5 AMP). God knows everything about us and is intimately familiar with all our thoughts. Nothing is hidden from Him. If you are living uprightly, you can derive comfort from knowing that God is aware of everything you do, including the motivations behind your actions. In fact, He knows you better than you know yourself. That is why David prayed,

> *You have searched me, LORD, and you know me. You know when I sit and when I rise; you perceive my thoughts from afar. You discern my going out and my lying down; you are familiar with all my ways.*
> (Psalm 139:1–3 NIV)

The Mysterious Three in One

When we try to understand God, we come up against a paradox. This God is one God, and Christianity is a monotheistic religion. Yet He is three at the same time. He is three in one: Father, Son, and Holy Spirit. The triune nature of the Godhead is one of the most profound mysteries of Christianity. How can God be unified and yet triune?

Over the centuries since Jesus' resurrection, people have struggled to understand this truth. Jesus was not only the Messiah but also the Son of God the Father, and He sent the Holy Spirit on the day of Pentecost, the birthday of the church. Since then, the church has discovered that it cannot get along with only one or two of the members of the Trinity—but, because They are three in one, it does not have to.

Each of the three distinct Persons of the Godhead is fully God. None is less than another. Yet these three Persons are only *one* God, not three equal "Gods." This simple truth is almost impossible for the finite human mind to grasp, and yet human hearts can believe it. How can God be described in terms of both unity and plurality? The church has struggled (especially in its first few hundred years) to define the Trinity clearly enough to overcome error and heresy. Unity and plurality must be held in perfect balance in order to maintain a correct view of God. Emphasizing the oneness of God at the expense of His three-ness will lead to error, and vice versa.

The theological term "the Trinity" is not found in Scripture, although the concept or principle is. Sometimes, we try to explain the Trinity by saying that God is like water in its three forms: liquid, steam, and ice. That illustration may help some people to get a better grip on the concept, but it falls flat in the long run. The same H_2O molecules alternate between appearing as liquid, steam, or ice, but the mode of existence depends on external factors. God's three Persons do not change and shift like that—sometimes behaving like the Father, sometimes the Son, and sometimes the Spirit. God is fully each Person, all the time, without changing.

Although no analogy works perfectly, think about the way your Bible is composed. It has sixty-six books, and yet it is only one Book. Any single book is not the whole Bible, but the Book is not whole without every one of the books. Each of the books is of equal biblical importance to the others. Likewise, with Father, Son, and Holy Spirit, none of the Three is any less than the Others.

Because He is typically listed last, the Holy Spirit is often relegated in many people's minds to being sort of a "junior partner," a lesser expression of God's personality or personhood. To hold such a view is a big mistake.

I have news for those who think in this way: The Holy Spirit knows He is God! And, *"where the Spirit of the Lord is, there is liberty"* (2 Corinthian 3:17). In fact, we each first meet the Holy Spirit on a personal level as He convinces us of our need for Jesus, but I will hold that concept for a later review. Part of the reason the Spirit is here with us is to run the church. Yes, our Father loves us and is Lord. Yes, Jesus loves us and is Lord. But the Holy Spirit also loves us, and He is Lord, as well. And when the church doesn't allow the Holy Spirit to have free rein, the body of Christ fails to experience the fullness of the kingdom of God. (Ouch! That one hurt—it is painfully true!)

In Unity, One

These ancient words say it best: *"Hear, O Israel: The LORD our God, the LORD is one!"* (Deuteronomy 6:4 NKJV).

When God brought the children of Israel out of Egypt, He called them away from the polytheism (worship of many gods) of Egypt and the surrounding nations, telling them that there was only one God in heaven—the God of Abraham, Isaac, and Jacob. This became a major theme throughout the books of the Old Testament: There are no gods but God alone. (See, for example, Isaiah 43:10; 45:5.) Archeological discoveries of ancient Egypt have revealed the Egyptians' worship of animals, the landscape, natural forces, the pharaohs, and more. The Israelites had been surrounded by false worship for their whole lives. Now God was telling them that it was utterly important not to worship idols, or other "gods"; not to hold these "gods" in higher esteem than they held Him, and not to belittle His name in any way. He gave Moses His "top-Ten" Commandments, which included these:

> *You shall have no other gods before Me. You shall not make for yourself an idol, or any likeness of what is in heaven above or on the earth beneath or in the water under the earth. You shall not worship them or serve them; for I, the LORD your God, am a jealous God, visiting the iniquity of the fathers on the children, on the third and the fourth generations of those who hate Me, but showing lovingkindness to thousands, to those who love Me and keep My commandments. You shall not take the name of the LORD your God in vain, for the*

LORD *will not leave him unpunished who takes His name in vain.*

(Exodus 20:3–7)

This is serious business. No other gods. No other worship. No denigration of the one God. Now, as then, God wants us to trust Him exclusively, and to demonstrate our trust in the one true God by keeping His commandments.

In John 17:3, God is called *"the only true God"* because all other gods are false. Paul wrote to the Corinthians who were concerned about eating food that had been offered to idols, *"We know that an idol is nothing (has no real existence) and that there is no God but one"* (1 Corinthians 8:4 AMP; see also Jeremiah 10:1–6, 16).

In Unity, Three

Yes, God is one. But the idea that this one God is plural is expressed as early as the first chapter of the Bible. Have you ever noticed the unusual use of the language there? *"Then God said, 'Let Us make man in Our image, according to Our likeness'"* (Genesis 1:26). The one God uses the plural terms *"Us"* and *"Our"*!

All three distinct Persons of the Godhead were present at Jesus' baptism. In the following account, we see the Son, Jesus, being empowered by the Holy Spirit, while the Father speaks His approval from heaven:

> *When all the people were being baptized, Jesus was baptized too. And as he was praying, heaven was opened and the Holy Spirit descended on him in bodily form like a dove. And a voice came from heaven: "You are my Son, whom I love; with you I am well pleased."*
>
> (Luke 3:21–22 NIV)

To reiterate: These three Persons of the Trinity—Father, Son, and Holy Spirit—are indeed Persons, not merely "manifestations" or "modes" of God. Jesus the Son was sent by the Father (see, for example, 1 John 4:10), and He returned to the Father (see, for example, John 3:13), at whose right hand He is now seated (see, for example, Mark 16:19). The Son sent the Spirit, who was promised by the Father, after Jesus ascended to heaven (see John 14:16–17, 20–23; Acts 2:33); and, after that, the Holy Spirit is mentioned frequently in the New Testament. (See, for example, Acts 13:1–3; Acts 15:28–29; 2 Corinthians 13:14.)

The single greatest desire of the Trinity is to see human beings reunited with God and with each other. Again, while He was on earth, Jesus prayed to the Father for His followers in these words:

> *The glory which You have given Me I have given to them, that they may*
> *be one, just as We are one; I in them and You in Me, that they may be*
> *perfected in unity, so that the world may know that You sent Me, and*
> *loved them, even as You have loved Me. Father, I desire that they also,*
> *whom You have given Me, be with Me where I am, so that they may*
> *see My glory which You have given Me, for You loved Me before the*
> *foundation of the world. O righteous Father, although the world has not*
> *known You, yet I have known You; and these have known that You*
> *sent Me; and I have made Your name known to them, and will make*
> *it known, so that the love with which You loved Me may be in them,*
> *and I in them.* (John 17:22–26)

One of the ways we know that each of the Persons within the Trinity must be fully God, and not merely a manifestation of the same God, is that manifestations don't converse with one another, make promises, express mutual affection, or undertake efforts and activities, as these Persons do. I wish we had a better term to use. "Person" is OK, but each Person of the Godhead is more than just a person. And God is not a triple personality, or a "multiple personality," either!

God is not divided; each of the members of the Trinity is unified with the others. Various Scriptures try to put this concept into words, such as the following: "*For in Him* [Jesus] *all the fullness of Deity dwells in bodily form*" (Colossians 2:9). Jesus is no less God than the Father Himself. (See, for example, John 1:1.) We see that Peter equated the Holy Spirit with God when he rebuked Ananias for lying to the Holy Spirit, saying, "*Ananias, why has Satan filled your heart to lie to the Holy Spirit…?…You have not lied to men but to God*" (Acts 5:3–4).

Earlier in this chapter, I defined God's omnipotence, His omnipresence, and His omniscience. Each of these major attributes is fully expressed by each Person of the Godhead. If we believe that God the Father is all-powerful, ever present, and all-knowing, and if we know that Jesus is the exact representation of the Father (see Hebrews 1:3), then Jesus is equal to the Father and has those attributes, as well. (When He became a Man and lived on the earth to be our Representative and the Sacrifice for our sin, Jesus voluntarily gave up some of His divine attributes, such as His omnipresence—but He never relinquished His divine nature. These attributes were restored to Him when He ascended to heaven after His triumphant resurrection.) Likewise, the Holy Spirit is equal to the Father. Jesus equated all three members of the Trinity with one another when He said, *"The Helper, the Holy Spirit, whom the Father will send in My name, He will teach you all things, and bring to your remembrance all that I said to you"* (John 14:26).

God's True Nature

To comprehend the vastness of God in even a partial way, we must approach Him repeatedly and from as many viewpoints as we can. Being humans, we always start, by default, by viewing God through a human lens. Eventually, we recognize the limitations of that approach, and we turn our attention to the member of the Trinity who looks the most like us—Jesus, who takes us further toward understanding the Divinity.

Jesus introduces us to the Holy Spirit, and vice versa; both provide us a direct encounter with God's love. Because God *is* love (see 1 John 4:8, 16), our experience of being washed repeatedly in His love opens our eyes to what He is really like, and then we never stop learning more about Him.

Now, don't get lost in all the theological technicalities! A contemporary Christian song is rising in my heart right now as I compose this: "I want to see Your face / I want to know You more"![5] Truly, knowing God intimately means knowing His heart attributes more than all the theological terminology.

---

*Jesus and the Holy Spirit alike provide us
a direct encounter with God's love.*

---

5. From "In the Secret," by Chris Tomlin.

Our Distorted Conceptions

In order to allow our perception of God's character to become rooted in a revelation of the love of God, we must abandon all our misconceptions about Him. This is what I had to do in relation to the warped view I grew up with concerning God as Father, which I discussed briefly in chapter 1 of this book. Until you see clearly how much God loves you, your concept of Him will be twisted and marred by fear, which is the opposite of love. (See 1 John 4:18–19.) You will never quite understand God's good intentions toward you. You will share the corrupted view of Him that Satan exploited in the garden of Eden in order to paint an erroneous picture of God to the first human beings. Let's make sure we get a clear and accurate picture of Him.

God created the first human beings so that they could have fellowship with Him, and, of course, they took that fellowship for granted. Then, after the devil persuaded them to sin, fear came into their lives. Now Adam and Eve tried to hide from God. (See Genesis 3:8–10.) They completely lost sight of the fact that He is a loving Father. As time went on, people grew even more afraid of God. Recall the terrified reaction of the Israelites to the manifestation of God's presence on Mount Sinai. (See Exodus 19.) They couldn't handle it, so they sent Moses to talk with God, while they stayed a safe distance away. What a pity such a reaction is, considering the way God would prefer to speak with each of us—heart to heart.

Satan's deceit spread like a plague. So, it is not surprising that when God's own Son came to earth many generations later, the devil found it easy to use people's distorted conceptions of God to his further advantage. Satan is the "god" of this world, as Paul wrote: "*The god of this world has blinded the minds of the unbelieving so that they might not see the light of the gospel of the glory of Christ, who is the image of God*" (2 Corinthians 4:4).

In the Person of Jesus Christ, God stood right in front of people, yet most of them were blind to the fact. They ignored Him or brushed Him off. Satan's original deception had been inbred for so long that nobody recognized God's love in the flesh. People had bought into the lie that God is a withholder, despite Scriptures that state the direct opposite, such as this one: "*For the LORD God is a sun and shield; the LORD bestows favor and honor; no good thing does he withhold from those whose walk is blameless"* (Psalm 84:11 NIV).

To this day, as we know all too well, the enemy's lies are denying people access to God's love. What can be done about it? Believers must settle in their own hearts and minds that God loves them, and that He is not holding out on them. The fact that the Father sent His own Son to die for us should be eternal, unfading proof that God is a liberal giver and not a withholder: *"He who did not spare His own Son, but delivered Him over for us all, how will He not also with Him freely give us all things?"* (Romans 8:32; see also 1 Corinthians 1:4–7).

Time-out!

Some of you might need to push the "pause" button before you proceed any further. God Himself wants to heal our minds and hearts from wounds that cause distortions in our understanding of who He is and what He is like. Just call on His name and ask Him to heal your heart and to clear your vision. He is more than willing to meet you right now—right where you are.

You see, it is far too easy for people to acquire a good intellectual understanding about God without building any kind of a relationship with Him. They may have received the gift of salvation from Him, but little else. They've got "religion," or a form of "churchianity," or even great "head knowledge" of God, but not authentic, heartfelt faith. Only by faith—which is a heart thing more than it is a head thing—can we know God. We are talking about having a passionate pursuit of God in response to the way He first passionately pursued us. For me, getting to know more of His amazing, approachable characteristics is learning to love Him more!

By faith, we can receive His love and express it to others. We don't want to become like the Samaritans who rejected Jesus and His disciples simply because they were headed to Jerusalem, which was "against their religion." And we don't want to become like the disciples who reacted to the Samaritans' rejection by asking Jesus if they could call down fire from heaven to incinerate them. (See Luke 9:52–56.)

The disciples did not yet understand the heart of the Father God, nor His reason for sending His Son. Instead, they projected onto Him their old ways of thinking and responding to people. The disciples (and the Samaritans) were operating out of a set of ideas about God formed largely by their cultural traditions instead of by the Word of God.

Today's believers are no different. That's why so many people carry an image of God as an angry ogre who is poised to strike down any offender without mercy—or the complete opposite, a wishy-washy, all-embracing Jesus who would never say a corrective word to anyone.

The most reliable sourcebook for what God is like is the Word of God itself, in which God warns us ahead of time,

> *My thoughts are not your thoughts, nor are your ways My ways....For as the heavens are higher than the earth, so are My ways higher than your ways and My thoughts than your thoughts.* (Isaiah 55:8–9)

Never, ever assume that you know what God is thinking unless He tells you through His Word. Presumption always leads to misunderstanding. And misunderstanding leads to conflict with our fellow believers, as we start dishonoring each other and arguing about our views of the truth. "Religion" has set back the cause of God. If we don't watch out, we will defame God's character as we insult each other in the name of religion and partial truth. The only one who's pleased with that is the devil. God is the Author of faith, hope, and love. Not competition, jealousy, and strife.

In fact, God lives in community! God *is* community. God likes Himself! Wow—now, that is an amazing concept to contemplate for a while. The three Persons of the Trinity are not threatened by one another. Each wants the other members to receive the glory! I imagine Them saying to each other, "You are so great!" "Actually, You are!" "But I cannot do what I do without You." God lives in a no-competition zone with Himself!

God's Image Revealed in His Son

In addition to the written Word, God's clearest expression to us of His nature comes in the form of His Son. Jesus Christ is God in the flesh, eating and drinking and teaching and healing—and offering Himself as a perfect Sacrifice so that we could know God for ourselves.

[Jesus] is the radiance of [God's] glory and the exact representation of His nature, and upholds all things by the word of His power. When He had made purification of sins, He sat down at the right hand of the Majesty on high, having become as much better than the angels, as He has inherited a more excellent name than they. (Hebrews 1:3–4)

Jesus exactly represents God and His great love for the people He has created in His image. Jesus is God's statement to the world, "Here I am! Here is what I am like!" In every way, Jesus exemplifies the love of God, not only through His words but also by His lifestyle of compassionate intervention.

The Shepherd came to rescue His sheep and to make sure that His rescue operation could continue until the end of time. When He walked the dusty roads of Judea, He spoke clearly about what His Father was like and how to approach Him, saying, for example:

Your Father who sees what is done in secret will reward you....And when you are praying, do not use meaningless repetition as the Gentiles do, for they suppose that they will be heard for their many words. So do not be like them; for your Father knows what you need before you ask Him. Pray, then, in this way: "Our Father who is in heaven, hallowed be Your name...." (Matthew 6:4, 7–9)

Ask and it will be given to you; seek and you will find; knock and the door will be opened to you....Which of you, if your son asks for bread, will give him a stone? Or if he asks for a fish, will give him a snake? If you, then, though you are evil, know how to give good gifts to your children, how much more will your Father in heaven give good gifts to those who ask him! (Matthew 7:7, 9–11 NIV)

The Father Himself loves you, because you have loved Me and have believed that I came forth from the Father. (John 16:27)

Throughout His earthly ministry, Jesus added actions to His words, exemplifying the Father's love by His deeds. Here is a peek at what He did during His short, three-year ministry:

You know of Jesus of Nazareth, how God anointed Him with the Holy Spirit and with power, and how He went about doing good and healing all who were oppressed by the devil, for God was with Him.

(Acts 10:38)

When He went ashore and saw a great throng of people, He had compassion (pity and deep sympathy) for them and cured their sick.

(Matthew 14:14 AMP)

Jesus called his disciples to him and said, "I have compassion for these people; they have already been with me three days and have nothing to eat. I do not want to send them away hungry, or they may collapse on the way."…Then [Jesus] took the seven loaves and the fish, and when he had given thanks, he broke them and gave them to the disciples, and they in turn to the people. They all ate and were satisfied. Afterward the disciples picked up seven basketfuls of broken pieces that were left over.   (Matthew 15:32, 36–37 NIV)

His disciples took it all in. After Jesus returned to heaven, they repeated His teaching until, by the inspiration of the Holy Spirit, much of it was written down in the form that we now call the Bible. And from the very beginning of the life of the church, they replicated His powerfully compassionate acts.

Knowing God's Heart of Love

We do not live in the first century. That was a long time ago. How can we twenty-first-century Christians not only experience God's love but also reproduce His compassionate acts, as Jesus' disciples did? Just knowing the historical facts and theological assertions isn't enough, is it?

The apostle Peter's words are just as true today as they were twenty-one hundred years ago:

His divine power has bestowed upon us all things that [are requisite and suited] to life and godliness, through the [full, personal] knowledge of Him Who called us by and to His own glory and excellence (virtue).   (2 Peter 1:3 AMP)

Read through that verse again, putting your own name in place of "*us.*" His divine power has been bestowed upon...whom? Upon you and me. Through what? Through knowing Him, personally knowing Him. How? By our "getting to know God and His Word"!

Too many people attempt to live a godly life under their own steam. For example, through the power of self-will, they may temporarily mask their sin and try to conquer their bad habits. But to live a truly consistent, godly lifestyle, we need His help. Band-Aids don't work for long! We need God in order to know God!

Our God is approachable. It is actually possible to know the One who generously gives to whoever asks. (See Luke 11:9–13.) You can learn to recognize His voice. You can know God and walk with Him. As you do, you will then (and only then) be able to appropriate all the gifts He has bestowed. He will grant you increasing knowledge of Him, a renewed mind, life-giving grace and kindness, and true transformation into His image. You can be changed!

Our God is approachable. You can know God and walk with Him.

From His Word, here's proof positive of His desire and promise to dwell with you and to remake you in His image:

> *May Christ through your faith [actually] dwell (settle down, abide, make His permanent home) in your hearts! May you be rooted deep in love and founded securely on love, that you may have the power and be strong to apprehend and grasp with all the saints [God's devoted people, the experience of that love] what is the breadth and length and height and depth [of it]; [that you may really come] to know [practically, through experience for yourselves] the love of Christ, which far surpasses mere knowledge [without experience]; that you may be filled [through all your being] unto all the fullness of God [may have the richest measure of the divine Presence, and become a body wholly filled and flooded with God Himself]!*
>
> (Ephesians 3:17–19 AMP)

> *But God, being rich in mercy, because of His great love with which He loved us, even when we were dead in our transgressions, made us alive together with Christ (by grace you have been saved), and raised us up with Him, and seated us with Him in the heavenly places in Christ Jesus, so that in the ages to come He might show the surpassing riches of His grace in kindness toward us in Christ Jesus.*
>
> (Ephesians 2:4–7)

> *Do not conform to the pattern of this world, but be transformed by the renewing of your mind. Then you will be able to test and approve what God's will is—his good, pleasing and perfect will.*
>
> (Romans 12:2 NIV)

God perfectly defines the word *love*. What an amazing love He demonstrates! He saves and rescues us from the darkness of sin, and He exercises His miracle-working power to liberate us and transform us and teach us to love. Truly, *"He is a rewarder of those who diligently seek Him"* (Hebrews 11:6 NKJV).

He does it perfectly. In one way, I wish that when I was born again, God had taken a scrub brush to my brain, scouring it clean. But He did not. Likewise, He leaves each of us a measure of "working out" our own salvation *"with fear and trembling"* (Philippians 2:12). He is a partner with us, and He has given us His Word, both as a promise and as a guide. He has given us the power of prayer. He has given us a community of believers. And, He has given us the gift of the Holy Spirit. Thus, best of all, He has given us Himself, so that we can keep being renewed from the first moment of our new life forward.

"And so we know and rely on the love God has for us. God is love. Whoever lives in love lives in God, and God in them" (1 John 4:16 NIV). Because, you see, *"there is no fear in love; but perfect love casts out fear, because fear involves punishment, and the one who fears is not perfected in love"* (1 John 4:18).

God gets to live His life through us, and we get to be continually renewed in the process.

"For we are made partakers of Christ, if we hold the beginning of our confidence stedfast unto the end" (Hebrews 3:14 KJV).

The Almighty, Loving Father

For too long, the church has been paralyzed by distorted views of God. But we are awakening to the fact that God is for us and will not hold out on us. The early church knew this reality better than we do, and they performed mighty works. Faithful believers over the centuries have been carried forward by the same truth. We can pick up where they left off—if we accept God's invitation to become rooted in His love and to grow in it. (See Ephesians 3:17–19.) *"We love, because He first loved us"* (1 John 4:19)!

As some of you know, I was a singer before I was ever a preacher or an author. So, songs rise in my heart all the time. Here comes another one: "How Great Is Our God"[6]! God is all-loving, all-knowing, ever present, and all-powerful. And, He is all-available to us through His Son Jesus and by the might and power of the Holy Spirit, as we apply what Jesus said: *"Truly, truly, I say to you, he who believes in Me, the works that I do, he will do also; and greater works than these he will do; because I go to the Father"* (John 14:12).

The more I know Him, the more I want to know Him. I am so hungry to know everything I can about this God who loves me. How about you? Are you growing in your pursuit of God?

---

6. Chris Tomlin, Ed Cash, and Jesse Reeves, 2004.

4

The Messiah Has Come!

Jesus said to him, "Have I been so long with you,
and yet you have not come to know Me, Philip?
He who has seen Me has seen the Father; how can you say,
'Show us the Father'?...No one comes to the Father but through Me."
—John 14:9, 6

It is important...that we should be clear in our minds as to what
knowing Jesus Christ means.[7]
—J. I. Packer

Jesus the rabbi had been walking all day in the company of the twelve young men who were His disciples. As they entered the region of Caesarea Philippi, they decided to take a short rest in the welcome shade by a spring-fed pool. Twenty miles back, they had left behind thousands of men, women, and children who had started following Jesus around the Sea of Galilee. Their rabbi was also a miracle-worker, and He had healed the lame, the deaf, and the blind, and had topped it off by feeding more than

7. J. I. Packer, *Knowing God* (Downers Grove, IL: InterVarsity Press, 1973), 37.

four thousand people by multiplying a meager supply of bread and fish. (See, for example, Matthew 15:29–39.)

"Who Do People Say That I Am?"

As the disciples rested their tired feet, Jesus turned to them and asked, point-blank, *"Who do people say that the Son of Man is?"* (Matthew 16:13; see also Mark 8:27).

Excited speculations about Jesus swirled among people in whatever locale He visited, so His disciples told Him, *"Some say John the Baptist; and others, Elijah; but still others, Jeremiah, or one of the prophets"* (Matthew 16:14). Why those three prophets, all of whom were dead, one of them only recently?

Most people knew that Herod, the ruler of Galilee, had beheaded John only a short time before. Were they thinking that Jesus was really John, brought back from the dead? If so, was it because the same crowds who had followed John were now following Jesus, and that His message resembled John's? Was it the miracles? That's what Herod thought: *"Herod the tetrarch heard the reports about Jesus, and he said to his attendants, 'This is John the Baptist; he has risen from the dead! That is why miraculous powers are at work in him'"* (Matthew 14:1–2 NIV).

Perhaps some of the people were hoping that Jesus was the Elijah who would fulfill Malachi's prophecy: *"Behold, I will send you Elijah the prophet before the great and terrible day of the Lord comes"* (Malachi 4:5 AMP). In their oral tradition, they would have rehearsed these words many times, speculating as to when and how they would be fulfilled.

Or, perhaps the people who said Jesus was really Jeremiah, otherwise known as "the weeping prophet," were basing their guess on Jesus' overflowing compassion for the people. If I had been among those crowds, I might have supposed that I was seeing a new Jeremiah or Elijah. It would have made sense.

"Who Do You Say That I Am?"

Then the Master shifted to a second question: *"But who do you say that I am?"* (Matthew 16:15).

Most of the men were not so quick to answer this time. They were not yet sure they knew. Obviously, this was a bigger question. To this day, it remains the greatest question that every single individual must answer.

But Peter, hardly hesitating, blurted out, *"You are the Christ, the Son of the living God"* (Matthew 16:16). And Jesus exclaimed, *"Blessed are you, Simon Barjona, because flesh and blood did not reveal this to you, but My Father who is in heaven"* (Matthew 16:17).

As I always say, "It takes God to know God," and I know that Peter could have recognized Jesus' divinity only with the help of God's Spirit. Without realizing who had put the idea into his head, Peter opened his mouth and spoke the truest thing he had ever uttered. Not to insult the one who became such a great apostle, but, prior to that moment, Peter had been a bit of a numbskull, almost like one of The Three Stooges. And then, suddenly, looming tall with apostolic authority, he announced to the others that their remarkable rabbi was really the *Christos* (Greek for "Christ," the Anointed One who was the true Messiah).

Jesus told Peter that his natural senses could not possibly have penetrated the mystery of His identity, and the same will always be true for any human being. The Spirit of revelation must show us who Jesus is. Then, like Peter, we can acknowledge that Jesus comes from the Father and that He is the Son of the living God. In other words, the first Person of the Godhead that anybody encounters must be the Spirit, because He opens the way to a life-changing meeting with the Son and the Father by convicting us concerning the spiritual realities of life.

The Son of the living God is the Messiah—the long-expected King and Deliverer of the Jews, and the Savior of all humankind. Once Jesus Christ is part of the picture in our lives, things change. The Jewish Messiah is the Christian Savior. Without Judaism, there would have been no Messiah. Without the Messiah, there could have been no Christianity. Without Jesus the Messiah, humankind would still be in darkness.

"Who do you say that I am?" Jesus confronts each one of us with that question. Our answer determines our present, our future, and our eternal destiny. This is the single most important question that every person must answer. Head knowledge is good, but you must know this Messiah Jesus

from your heart. That is what an authentic relationship is all about—an engaged heart. So, who do you say in your heart that Jesus Christ is?

Our answer to Jesus' question "Who do you say that I am?" determines our present, our future, and our eternal destiny.

Jesus, Fulfiller of Messianic Prophecy

We can find at least 129 biblical prophecies concerning the first advent (coming) of the Messiah, Christ Jesus—His coming to earth as a baby and His ministry. As Acts 3:24 accurately states, *"Yes, and all the prophets, from Samuel and those who follow, as many as have spoken, have also foretold these days"* (NKJV). Twice that number of additional Old Testament prophecies also talk about Christ's second advent. I will not be able to do more than scratch the surface of the full number of Old Testament passages that correlate with their fulfillment in the New Testament. Yet let's take a few steps on this enlightening journey together of getting to know God and His Word.

Prophecies of the Messiah's Birth

Born of a Virgin

Isaiah boldly prophesied that God would send a Son, and that He would be conceived in the womb of a young woman who had never had sexual intercourse: *"The Lord Himself will give you a sign: behold, the virgin shall conceive and bear a Son, and shall call His name Immanuel"* (Isaiah 7:14 NKJV). He got it exactly right. What happened? A young woman—just a teenager, really—named Mary in the town of Nazareth, who was betrothed to an older man named Joseph but was still living with her parents, had a startling visit from the archangel Gabriel. Luke and Matthew give us these accounts:

> *God sent the angel Gabriel to Nazareth, a town in Galilee, to a virgin pledged to be married to a man named Joseph, a descendant of David. The virgin's name was Mary.* (Luke 1:26–27 NIV)

Now the birth of Jesus Christ took place under these circumstances: When His mother Mary had been promised in marriage to Joseph, before they came together, she was found to be pregnant [through the power] of the Holy Spirit....All this took place that it might be fulfilled which the Lord had spoken through the prophet, Behold, the virgin shall become pregnant and give birth to a Son, and they shall call His name Emmanuel—which, when translated, means, God with us....But he had no union with her as her husband until she had borne her firstborn Son; and he called His name Jesus. (Matthew 1:18, 22–23, 25 AMP)

The Son of God was born to a virgin mother, to a young woman who had never known a man. Just ponder this one prophetic revelation alone. As you do, it will create wonder and awe in your heart. Oh, the majesty and exquisite planning of God!

Born in Bethlehem

Even the name of the village where Mary would give birth to the Messiah appeared in prophecy. Micah got that one:

But you, Bethlehem Ephrathah, though you are little among the thousands of Judah, yet out of you shall come forth to Me the One to be Ruler in Israel, whose goings forth are from of old, from everlasting. (Micah 5:2 NKJV)

It wasn't Nazareth, as you might expect, but Bethlehem, about seventy miles away, that was the Messiah's birthplace. This occurred because of special circumstances, which both Luke and Matthew record. Let us look first at the passage from Luke:

In those days Caesar Augustus issued a decree that a census should be taken of the entire Roman world. (This was the first census that took place while Quirinius was governor of Syria.) And everyone went to their own town to register. So Joseph also went up from the town of Nazareth in Galilee to Judea, to Bethlehem the town of David, because he belonged to the house and line of David. He went there to register with Mary, who was pledged to be married to him and was expecting a child. (Luke 2:1–5 NIV)

In order to fulfill the prophecies, Jesus needed to come from the lineage of King David, which Joseph, the humble carpenter, did, as did Mary, his betrothed. The inconvenient census caused Joseph and Mary to travel to another part of the country, where the descendants of David were supposed to register.

Even King Herod (father of Herod Antipas, who beheaded John the Baptist) took Micah's prophecy seriously, after he became concerned that it may have been fulfilled. He inquired of his best-informed scholars as to exactly where this *"Ruler"* was supposed to be born.

> *Gathering together all the chief priests and scribes of the people, he inquired of them where the Messiah was to be born. They said to him, "In Bethlehem of Judea; for this is what has been written by the prophet: 'And you, Bethlehem, land of Judah, are by no means least among the leaders of Judah; for out of you shall come forth a Ruler who will shepherd My people Israel.'"* (Matthew 2:4–6)

A Son Shall Be Born

The prophecies were detailed about everything: This baby would be born to a virgin who would go into labor in the village of Bethlehem. And, the baby would be a boy, a Son. The prophets might have predicted that an angel would be coming to earth, or that a daughter would be born, or just "a child"—with no designation of gender. But Isaiah narrowed it down to a male Child, and he gave the Child many names to show His importance to the world:

> *For unto us a Child is born, unto us a Son is given; and the government will be upon His shoulder. And His name will be called Wonderful, Counselor, Mighty God, Everlasting Father, Prince of Peace.* (Isaiah 9:6 NKJV)

Once again, Matthew and Luke wrote about how the prophecy was fulfilled:

> [An angel of the Lord told Joseph,] "[Mary] *will give birth to a son, and you are to give him the name Jesus, because he will save his people*

*from their sins.".…[Joseph] did not consummate their marriage until
she gave birth to a son. And he gave him the name Jesus.*

(Matthew 1:21, 25 NIV)

[The angel Gabriel said to Mary,] *"You will conceive and give birth to
a son, and you are to call him Jesus. He will be great and will be called
the Son of the Most High. The Lord God will give him the throne of
his father David.…".…And she gave birth to her firstborn, a son. She
wrapped him in cloths and placed him in a manger, because there was
no guest room available for them.* (Luke 1:31–32; 2:7 NIV)

This was more than just another "gender reveal." And, the announcement "The Savior has come!" is more than a mere phrase on a Christmas
card. It is a living reality. Jesus, who is God, took on human flesh in order
to dwell among us!

After the angel Gabriel told Mary that she would bear a Son, he specified exactly what she should name Him: *"Jesus"* (Luke 1:31). Although *Jesus*
(*Yeshua*, or *Joshua*) was a fairly common name in those days, it means "God
saves," which turned out to be a pretty significant name for the Messiah,
the One who would save people from their sins.

Slaughter of the Little Children

It wasn't long before Herod caught up with Joseph, Mary, and Jesus—
or thought he had. To eliminate any chance that a child could grow up to
rival him, he sent soldiers to tear out of their mothers' arms all male babies
under the age of two, and to kill them with their blood-spattered swords.
Can you imagine the anguished grief of those mothers and their families?
Jeremiah had prophesied,

*This is what the LORD says: "A voice is heard in Ramah, mourning
and great weeping, Rachel weeping for her children and refusing to be
comforted, because they are no more."* (Jeremiah 31:15 NIV)

By the time of Herod's slaughter, Jesus and His parents were far away
in Egypt, Joseph having been warned in a dream to flee. (See Matthew
2:13–14.) But the weeping prophet's word had been fulfilled:

> *Then when Herod saw that he had been tricked by the magi, he became*
> *very enraged, and sent and slew all the male children who were in*
> *Bethlehem and all its vicinity, from two years old and under, according*
> *to the time which he had determined from the magi. Then what had*
> *been spoken through Jeremiah the prophet was fulfilled:* **"A voice was**
> **heard in Ramah, weeping and great mourning, Rachel weeping for**
> **her children;** *and she refused to be comforted, because they were no*
> *more."*   (Matthew 2:16–18)

The *"Rachel"* symbolized in Jeremiah's prophecy was Jacob's wife, the
one who died in childbirth. She died at Ramah (located in the region that
later became the territory of Benjamin) while traveling south from Bethel
to Bethlehem with Jacob and the rest of the family. (See Genesis 35:16–20.)
The prophet Samuel referred to Rachel's tomb as being in that area. (See
1 Samuel 10:2.) You could say that "Rachel's weeping" is still being heard
in Ramah. Less than four miles away from the modern-day location of
Ramah (now called Er Ram) is the town of Ramallah, where the headquar-
ters of the Palestine Liberation Organization (PLO), the governing body of
Palestine, is located. The devil hates the place of Jesus' birth and has made
the area a violent home to the voice of conflict, peril, and death, apparently
not caring that this outcome, in itself, continues to fulfill prophecy.

Prophecies of the Messiah's Ministry of Teaching and Miracles

Moving on to prophecies concerning Jesus' ministry after He grew
up, here again, I can only choose a representative sampling. Many, many
prophecies speak in detail about His teachings and miracles. It always
makes my heart melt with love for Him to read about His compassion
toward people in need.

Healing Blind Eyes, Opening Deaf Ears

In Isaiah's prophecy about the Messiah, the prophet predicted, *"The*
eyes of the blind will be opened" (Isaiah 35:5). Jesus' followers recollected
these words as His ministry got underway and the words started to see

fulfillment. One of the most memorable of such healings occurred in Jericho, where a blind beggar named Bartimaeus (who must have been known by name to many in that locality) learned that Jesus of Nazareth would be passing by. Somehow—whether because of the excited buzz of the passersby, or possibly just because his other senses, including his spiritual discernment, were heightened due to his great deficit in eyesight—Bartimaeus knew that this was going to be his big chance. Turning his sightless eyes in the direction of the road, he cried out,

> "Jesus, Son of David, have mercy on me!" Many were sternly telling him to be quiet, but he kept crying out all the more, "Son of David, have mercy on me!" And Jesus stopped and said, "Call him here." So they called the blind man, saying to him, "Take courage, stand up! He is calling for you." Throwing aside his cloak, he jumped up and came to Jesus. And answering him, Jesus said, "What do you want Me to do for you?" And the blind man said to Him, "Rabboni, I want to regain my sight!" And Jesus said to him, "Go; your faith has made you well." Immediately he regained his sight and began following Him on the road. (Mark 10:47–52)

Blind Bartimaeus did not care what other people thought or said. He was going to grab healing while it might be available. He was going to shout loudly enough to be heard over the crowd's noise level. Beggars are never worried about social protocol. And his bold request was fully granted. From then on, I'm sure he never begged another day of his life.

Not only did Isaiah say that the miracle-working Messiah would open blind eyes, but the prophet added that He would also open deaf ears: "*The ears of the deaf will be unstopped*" (Isaiah 35:5). Often, when someone cannot hear, he cannot speak, either. If someone has been deaf since birth, he does not know what a human voice sounds like. Jesus encountered a deaf-mute boy whose concerned father was just as persistent as Bartimaeus was. When Jesus appeared, this father called out from the midst of the crowd. Evidently, Jesus' disciples had not been able to help him. (See Mark 9:18.) The father explained the situation: "*Teacher, I brought You my son, possessed with a spirit which makes him mute*" (Mark 9:17).

Jesus did not have any trouble identifying and eliminating the offending unclean spirit, thus healing both the boy's deafness and his muteness. What a miracle!

> *When Jesus saw that a crowd was rapidly gathering, He rebuked the unclean spirit, saying to it, "You deaf and mute spirit, I command you, come out of him and do not enter him again." After crying out and throwing him into terrible convulsions, it came out; and the boy became so much like a corpse that most of them said, "He is dead!" But Jesus took him by the hand and raised him; and he got up.*
>
> (Mark 9:25–27)

When Jesus set the boy free from deafness and muteness, He removed the blockage from his spirit, as well. Now he could grow up as a normal human being, free to pursue a livelihood and, I expect, to tell for the rest of his life about the day Jesus came to town. Never again would he suffer in mute terror as his body went out of control, flailing then rigid.

This same Jesus ministers to us today, whether or not we are being physically seized by an unclean spirit.[8] When our spirits are bound and gagged and paralyzed, unable to reach Jesus with faith, He needs only to speak a few words, and all our bonds fall off. Immediately, we can think clearly again. We are free to respond, because we can hear His words. Jesus is alive and well on planet Earth, and He is the same yesterday, today, and forever! (See Hebrews 13:8.)

Beggars are never worried about social protocol.
Blind Bartimaeus' bold request was fully granted by Jesus.

Teaching in Parables

I have only begun to pull out the Old Testament prophecies that Jesus fulfilled. One that is mentioned less frequently than others is this: *"I will open my mouth in a parable"* (Psalm 78:2).

---

8. For more detail on this subject, see James Goll, *Deliverance from Darkness* (Grand Rapids, MI: Chosen Books, 2010).

Who almost always opened His mouth to speak parables? The Messiah, Yeshua. After recording some of His teaching, Matthew reported, "*All these things Jesus spoke to the multitude in parables; and without a parable He did not speak to them, that it might be fulfilled which was spoken by the prophet, saying: 'I will open My mouth in parables; I will utter things kept secret from the foundation of the world'*" (Matthew 13:34–35 NKJV).

This was Jesus' ministry style, and it made Him able to teach truth with many layers of meaning that could reach many different people. What a brilliant Teacher. He speaks truth; He hides truth. By teaching in veiled parables, He creates an earnest longing within us in order to draw us into a passionate pursuit of God Himself.

Jesus told parables about prayer, redemption, love, forgiveness, wickedness, and the end of the world—as well as parables about seeking after God and growing in Him, which is what we are doing through this book. Truly, better than anyone before or since, Jesus fulfilled the psalmist's prophetic line "*I will open my mouth in a parable.*"

Proclaiming the Good News

The prophets knew that the Messiah would proclaim the "good news," although nobody could anticipate what His complete message would entail. And they knew that someone special—a "messenger"—would appear beforehand to clear the way for Him. Both Isaiah and Malachi spoke of this messenger:

> *A voice is calling, "Clear the way for the LORD in the wilderness; make smooth in the desert a highway for our God. Let every valley be lifted up, and every mountain and hill be made low; and let the rough ground become a plain, and the rugged terrain a broad valley."*
>
> (Isaiah 40:3–4)

> *"Behold, I send My messenger, and he will prepare the way before Me. And the Lord, whom you seek, will suddenly come to His temple, even the Messenger of the covenant, in whom you delight. Behold, He is coming," says the LORD of hosts.* (Malachi 3:1 NKJV)

They pictured a forerunner, a messenger, who would be long expected (in part due to their prophecies). Then, *"the Lord, whom you seek, [would] suddenly come to His temple,"* as Malachi had predicted. He did—and He still does.

We pray and seek God and expect His presence; and yet, when He shows up, we are startled and astonished. The believers who waited for the Spirit in the upper room could never have imagined that He would come in the way He did on the day of Pentecost. (See Acts 2.) How quickly the good news gets disseminated once the Chief Messenger shows up! (If you want to energize your faith, do a Bible study on the "suddenlies" of God.)

At the beginning of his gospel, Mark quoted the prophecy from Isaiah 40 in relation to John the Baptist. He wanted to make sure everyone understood that the fulfillment of that word had come in the flesh:

> *As it is written in Isaiah the prophet: "Behold, I send My messenger ahead of You, who will prepare Your way; the voice of one crying in the wilderness, 'Make ready the way of the Lord, make His paths straight.'" John the Baptist appeared in the wilderness preaching a baptism of repentance for the forgiveness of sins.* (Mark 1:2–4)

Preaching to the Poor

When Jesus appeared on the scene, where did He go first? To kings' palaces or governors' halls? No, He went wherever His feet could take Him, and He stopped along the way again and again to bless the poorest and most helpless ones. He is the original One who stopped for the one. He expressed the Father's love to those who were poor and helpless in the most fitting and "real" ways: healing their diseases, feeding their hungry stomachs, binding up their broken hearts—just as Isaiah had prophesied seven hundred years earlier:

> *The Spirit of the Sovereign LORD is on me, because the LORD has anointed me to proclaim good news to the poor. He has sent me to bind up the brokenhearted, to proclaim freedom for the captives and release from darkness for the prisoners.* (Isaiah 61:1 NIV)

His heart for the poor was bigger than anyone had ever seen before. All the other "messiahs" who had claimed to have been sent from God seemed to be concerned mostly with preaching against wickedness and/or stimulating political action. Jesus was different. He genuinely loved the people. He stopped what He was doing to gather children into His lap (see Matthew 19:13–15) and to make more than enough bread and fish for His hungry followers to eat (see, for example, John 6:1–14). He stopped a funeral procession in order to restore a widow's only son to life. (See Luke 7:11–17.) More often than not, His preaching took the form of compassionate action.

Jesus knew that He was fulfilling Isaiah's words. Early in His ministry, He visited the synagogue in His hometown, Nazareth, and was offered an opportunity to read publicly from the Scriptures.

And He came to Nazareth, where He had been brought up; and as was His custom, He entered the synagogue on the Sabbath, and stood up to read. And the book of the prophet Isaiah was handed to Him. And He opened the book and found the place where it was written, "The Spirit of the Lord is upon Me, because He anointed Me to preach the gospel to the poor. He has sent Me to proclaim release to the captives, and recovery of sight to the blind, to set free those who are oppressed, to proclaim the favorable year of the Lord." And He closed the book, gave it back to the attendant and sat down; and the eyes of all in the synagogue were fixed on Him. And He began to say to them, "Today this Scripture has been fulfilled in your hearing." (Luke 4:16–21)

He "proclaim[ed] *release to the captives*" openly, in spite of the negative reactions of the authorities and of the ordinary people who were rattled by His unprecedented deeds. Who was this Man? He could set the most hopeless captive free, such as the Gerasene demoniac:

When He got out of the boat, immediately a man from the tombs with an unclean spirit met Him, and he had his dwelling among the tombs. And no one was able to bind him anymore, even with a chain; because he had often been bound with shackles and chains, and the chains had been torn apart by him and the shackles broken in pieces, and no one was strong enough to subdue him....Seeing Jesus from a distance, he ran up and bowed down before Him; and shouting with a loud voice, he said, "What business do we have with each other, Jesus, Son of the Most High God? I implore You by God, do not torment me!" For He had been saying to him, "Come out of the man, you unclean spirit!" And He was asking him, "What is your name?" And he said to Him, "My name is Legion; for we are many."....And the people came to see what it was that had happened. They came to Jesus and observed the man who had been demon-possessed sitting down, clothed and in his right mind, the very man who had had the "legion"; and they became frightened....And they began to implore Him to leave their region.

(Mark 5:2–4, 6–9, 14–15, 17)

Jesus kept going, disregarding criticism. He knew another prophetic psalm that spoke of Him: *"Zeal for Your house has eaten me up, and the reproaches of those who reproach You have fallen on me"* (Psalm 69:9 NKJV). At one point, His disciples recalled that Scripture: *"Then His disciples remembered that it was written, 'Zeal for Your house has eaten Me up'"* (John 2:17 NKJV).

During His ministry, Jesus was passionate about whatever He did; that's because He is such a *Lover*. He loves people, especially downtrodden ones—the poor, the oppressed, the captives.

My dear late wife, Michal Ann Goll, received a revelation concerning the Lord's heart of mercy. She founded a ministry that continues to this day to touch the poor of the earth, for whom Jesus died. It is aptly named Compassion Acts. May we each embody this character of the nature of Christ in our own life in a personal manner. We must answer the profound question "What would Jesus do?"

Jesus loves people, especially downtrodden ones—the poor, the oppressed, the captives.

Riding on a Donkey

We are accustomed to hearing the Gospel accounts about Jesus, as well as the prophetic words that apply to Him, to the point that we fail to recognize how unusual some of the prophetic words are. Here is one example:

> *Rejoice greatly, Daughter Zion! Shout, Daughter Jerusalem! See, your king comes to you, righteous and victorious, lowly and riding on a donkey, on a colt, the foal of a donkey.* (Zechariah 9:9 NIV)

Who would prophesy that a king (*the* King) would choose such a humble means of transport? How much more specific can Zechariah be? And then, of course, it happened exactly as prophesied:

> *This took place to fulfill what was spoken through the prophet: "Say to Daughter Zion, 'See, your king comes to you, gentle and riding on a donkey, and on a colt, the foal of a donkey.'" The disciples went and did as Jesus had instructed them. They brought the donkey and the colt and placed their cloaks on them for Jesus to sit on.* (Matthew 21:4–7 NIV)

This scene in Jesus' life is often called "the Triumphal Entry," but I think it should be called "the Humble Entry." Conquering kings don't enter cities riding bareback on a young donkey. Wouldn't you expect a victorious and proud king to parade through the city gate on the back of a stallion, as trumpets sounded? But this King came in the opposite spirit, with no arrogance at all. That's why some people failed to see or recognize Him. The entire life and ministry of Jesus was a crosscurrent to the pompous ways of man—and still is—and we love Him for it. Being prophetic, Jesus walked against the flow of the world and its ways. Now, I can follow Someone like that!

The Friend's Betrayal

It moves me greatly to notice the intricacies of the prophetic words, and how completely they were fulfilled, down to the last detail. Communing in worship with God, the psalmist wrote, *"Even my own familiar friend in whom I trusted, who ate my bread, has lifted up his heel against me"* (Psalm 41:9 NKJV). What happened ten centuries later? The word was fulfilled, down to the last detail—even the part about the bread.

After he had said this, Jesus was troubled in spirit and testified, "Very truly I tell you, one of you is going to betray me." His disciples stared at one another, at a loss to know which of them he meant. One of them, the disciple whom Jesus loved, was reclining next to him. Simon Peter motioned to this disciple and said, "Ask him which one he means." Leaning back against Jesus, he asked him, "Lord, who is it?" Jesus answered, "It is the one to whom I will give this piece of bread when I have dipped it in the dish." Then, dipping the piece of bread, he gave it to Judas, the son of Simon Iscariot. As soon as Judas took the bread, Satan entered into him. So Jesus told him, "What you are about to do, do quickly." But no one at the meal understood why Jesus said this to him. (John 13:21–28 NIV)

Already, Judas had bargained with the chief priests—for a specified price of thirty pieces of silver—to hand Jesus over to them. Thirty pieces of silver. Not twenty-five. Not gold, but silver. It sounds familiar, especially when you look at these two passages side by side:

Then I said to them, "If it is agreeable to you, give me my wages; and if not, refrain." So they weighed out for my wages thirty pieces of silver. And the LORD said to me, "Throw it to the potter"—that princely price they set on me. So I took the thirty pieces of silver and threw them into the house of the LORD for the potter. (Zechariah 11:12–13 NKJV)

Then one of the twelve, named Judas Iscariot, went to the chief priests and said, "What are you willing to give me to betray Him to you?" And they weighed out thirty pieces of silver to him. From then on he began looking for a good opportunity to betray Jesus. (Matthew 26:14–16)

In addition, the word *"potter"* catches your attention when you read what Zechariah prophesied, particularly if you recognize its connection with the thirty pieces of silver and Judas:

Then when Judas, who had betrayed Him, saw that He had been condemned, he felt remorse and returned the thirty pieces of silver to the chief priests and elders, saying, "I have sinned by betraying innocent blood." But they said, "What is that to us? See to that yourself!" And he threw the pieces of silver into the temple sanctuary and departed; and he went away and hanged himself. The chief priests took the pieces of silver and said, "It is not lawful to put them into the temple treasury, since it is the price of blood." And they conferred together and with the money bought the Potter's Field as a burial place for strangers.

(Matthew 27:3–7)

The precise coordination between the prophetic words and the actual circumstances surrounding the Messiah's betrayal is simply mind-boggling.

Coming Attractions

Studying all the prophetic passages of Scripture concerning the Messiah, and their fulfillment, can take a long time, because there are so many of them. Many additional prophetic words about Jesus have been fulfilled—about three hundred altogether. We will explore some of them in the next chapter. It makes me trust God's Word even more thoroughly when I see how intricately constructed it is, how marvelously every "jot and tittle" of the prophecies that were spoken about the Messiah have been (or will be) fulfilled in Jesus of Nazareth.

Just rereading the above selection of prophecies about the Word becoming flesh and dwelling among us makes me reflect with wonder and joy on the magnitude of God's plan. A whisper of gratitude rises from deep inside me and grows into a shout of praise for this God who makes Himself known to us in small and great ways, every day of our lives.

5

Wonderful Messiah, Son of God

What is more difficult to believe—that Jesus is God,
or that God became a man? One is as difficult to believe as the
other; in fact, one is as impossible to believe as the other—
except by the work of the Holy Spirit.[9]
—R. T. Kendall

When it comes to learning about how Messiah Jesus fulfills every one of the hundreds of ancient prophecies about Him, the challenge is not in understanding the words, which are utterly clear and specific. The challenge comes in comprehending all the material.

In the previous chapter, I pulled out a handful of prophetic words that had to do with Jesus' birth, His ministry, and His betrayal by Judas. Now we will press on to uncover a few more of the roughly three hundred prophecies that find their direct fulfillment in Jesus' life, death, and resurrection. The more we find out about Jesus, the more we know about God—and the more we want to know. As we feed our appetite, our appetite increases. So, let's pull up to the table for another serving of God's delightful Word.

---

9. R. T. Kendall, *Imitating Christ* (Lake Mary, FL: Charisma House, 2007), 52.

The Suffering of the Messiah

Jesus, having been betrayed by Judas into the hands of His enemies, suffered mercilessly. On top of being abused physically, He was abused verbally by both the soldiers and the people in the jeering crowd who watched the spectacle on the day of His crucifixion.

David prophesied in Psalm 22 that the Messiah would be thoroughly scorned:

> *But I am a worm, and no man; a reproach of men, and despised by the people. All those who see Me ridicule Me; they shoot out the lip, they shake the head, saying, "He trusted in the LORD, let Him rescue Him; let Him deliver Him, since He delights in Him!"*
>
> (Psalm 22:6–8 NKJV)

Today, we might say that David got a "download" from heaven when he wrote those words (and the words of his psalm that follows, which I will be quoting as the chapter goes on). Surely, the people who ranted at Jesus did not know that they were mocking God Himself. Matthew described the scene:

> *And those who passed by blasphemed Him, wagging their heads and saying, "You who destroy the temple and build it in three days, save Yourself! If You are the Son of God, come down from the cross." Likewise the chief priests also, mocking with the scribes and elders, said, "He saved others; Himself He cannot save. If He is the King of Israel, let Him now come down from the cross, and we will believe Him."*
>
> (Matthew 27:39–42 NKJV)

It looked like a bitter end to a false hope. But God had a plan, and the crucifixion was its centerpiece. He had been telling the prophets of Israel for centuries what to expect. In Peter's Pentecost sermon a couple of months later, the apostle declared,

> *Fellow Israelites, listen to this: Jesus of Nazareth was a man accredited by God to you by miracles, wonders and signs, which God did among you through him, as you yourselves know. This man was handed over*

to you by God's deliberate plan and foreknowledge; and you, with the
help of wicked men, put him to death by nailing him to the cross.

(Acts 2:22–23 NIV)

Jesus' death looked like a bitter end to a false hope.
But God had a plan, and the crucifixion was its centerpiece.

Did you know that the Romans used crucifixion as a means of execution for only about a hundred and thirty years? They started crucifying people approximately sixty years before Jesus' death on the cross, and they suspended the practice about seventy years later, having decided it was inhumane. This means that every prophecy that has to do with Jesus' suffering on the cross—and there are many of them—had to have been fulfilled during that relatively brief window of time. The prophetic descriptions of the torture are far more precise than you would expect them to be, covering everything from how He would look as a result of the harsh maltreatment to the fact that His clothing would be divided up by lot between His executioners.

Let's check out some of the most remarkable of the correlations between the prophecies and their fulfillment.

Prophecies of Jesus' Death

Pierced Through

On what is commonly known and commemorated as Good Friday, churches around the globe often quote three prophetic passages about the crucifixion, selecting these words of Isaiah and Zechariah, as well as a portion of Psalm 22, written by David:

He is despised and rejected by men, a Man of sorrows and acquainted
with grief. And we hid, as it were, our faces from Him; He was de-
spised, and we did not esteem Him. (Isaiah 53:3 NKJV)

And I will pour on the house of David and on the inhabitants of Jerusalem the Spirit of grace and supplication; then they will look on Me whom they pierced. Yes, they will mourn for Him as one mourns for his only son, and grieve for Him as one grieves for a firstborn.

(Zechariah 12:10 NKJV)

For dogs have surrounded me; a band of evildoers has encompassed me; they pierced my hands and my feet.   (Psalm 22:16)

If only Isaiah, Zechariah, and David could have seen the fulfillment of their words, when the Messiah was pierced as they had prophesied He would be:

But one of the soldiers pierced His side with a spear, and immediately blood and water came out.   (John 19:34)

Now Thomas, called the Twin, one of the twelve, was not with them when Jesus came. The other disciples therefore said to him, "We have seen the Lord." So he said to them, "Unless I see in His hands the print of the nails, and put my finger into the print of the nails, and put my hand into His side, I will not believe." And after eight days His disciples were again inside, and Thomas with them. Jesus came, the doors being shut, and stood in the midst, and said, "Peace to you!" Then He said to Thomas, "Reach your finger here, and look at My hands; and reach your hand here, and put it into My side. Do not be unbelieving, but believing."   (John 20:24–27 NKJV)

Did you know that your name is written in the imprints of His nail-pierced hands? Jesus stands all day long with His arms and hands outstretched to the people He loves. "Oh, how He loves you and me...."[10]

None of His Bones Broken

The crucifixion of Jesus, who is also known as the Lamb of God, occurred during the Passover Feast, and it mirrored the original Passover at the time of the exodus from Egypt. Back then, each Israelite household had been instructed to eliminate leavening from their baking, and to sacrifice

10. Kurt Kaiser, "Oh, How He Loves You and Me," 1975.

a lamb, daubing some of its fresh blood on the doorframe of their house. When the angel of death saw the sign of blood on their doorposts and lintels, he would pass over their house, and they would be saved from the plague of death.

God instructed Moses to tell the people not to break the bones of any of the slaughtered Passover lambs.

> *In one house it shall be eaten; you shall not carry any of the flesh outside the house, nor shall you break one of its bones.* (Exodus 12:46 NKJV)

In the same way, when the Lamb of God was sacrificed on the cross, none of His bones was broken.

> *He guards all his bones; not one of them is broken.*
> (Psalm 34:20 NKJV)

> *So the soldiers came, and broke the legs of the first man and of the other who was crucified with Him; but coming to Jesus, when they saw that He was already dead, they did not break His legs.* (John 19:32–33)

> *Purge out the old leaven, that you may be a new lump, since you truly are unleavened. For indeed Christ, our Passover, was sacrificed for us.*
> (1 Corinthians 5:7 NKJV)

Jesus, the Passover Lamb, was slain for our salvation, as foreshadowed in the Passover in Egypt. The Old Testament gives us many glimpses of what is to come in the New Testament, where its prophecies were literally fulfilled: salvation, cleansing, forgiveness, eternal life, healing, deliverance, and more.

Divided Garments

So many of the prophetic words about the Messiah were fulfilled by the actions of Jesus' enemies that nobody can argue that people who happened to know the prophecies were only performing as expected. Many of His enemies wouldn't have known what the prophets had said, least of all the Roman soldiers. Yet look at the prophecies they fulfilled:

They divide My garments among them, and for My clothing they cast lots.   (Psalm 22:18 NKJV)

Then they crucified Him, and divided His garments, casting lots, that it might be fulfilled which was spoken by the prophet: "They divided My garments among them, and for My clothing they cast lots."
                                          (Matthew 27:35 NKJV)

In the divine exchange that took place on the cross, Jesus bore our shame by hanging naked on a tree on that heaven-rending day. The more I know about Him, the more I want to learn.

Marred More than Any Other Man

The acclaimed movie *The Passion of the Christ* provides us with a graphic depiction of the scourging borne by our Messiah. But even the best movies ever produced about Christ's life hardly touch the depth of what Jesus endured on the cross.

Isaiah pictured the Suffering Servant as being lifted up (as was Jesus on the cross), after having been beaten and abused until His swollen, lacerated face was unrecognizable.

Behold, My Servant shall deal prudently; He shall be exalted and extolled and be very high. Just as many were astonished at you, so His visage was marred more than any man, and His form more than the sons of men.   (Isaiah 52:13–14 NKJV)

I gave My back to those who struck Me, and My cheeks to those who plucked out the beard; I did not hide My face from shame and spitting.   (Isaiah 50:6 NKJV)

The prophet Micah wrote, "*They will strike the judge of Israel with a rod on the cheek*" (Micah 5:1 NKJV). In precise fulfillment, the mocking soldiers smote Jesus with a rod:

They stripped him and put a scarlet robe on him, and then twisted together a crown of thorns and set it on his head. They put a staff in his right hand. Then they knelt in front of him and mocked him. "Hail, king of the Jews!" they said. They spit on him, and took the staff and struck him on the head again and again. After they had mocked him, they took off the robe and put his own clothes on him. Then they led him away to crucify him.   (Matthew 27:28–31 NIV)

Jesus suffered such extreme brutality because He was the ultimate scapegoat, carrying away all human sins for all time. (See Leviticus 16:8–26.) And He did this all for love's sake. This is the heart of God beating for the entire world to see.

Jesus exclaimed, *"It is finished!"* (John 19:30), and then He expired. This phrase declared that the work of the cross was perfect and complete. Nothing needs to be added to it, because the Son of God, who was also the Son of Man, accomplished it all on a bare hill where an old rugged cross stood like a sentinel.

Prophecies of Jesus' Burial and Resurrection

Even after Jesus died, the words of the prophets kept on being fulfilled. Joseph of Arimathea, a well-to-do member of the ruling religious council, who was a secret believer, requested Jesus' body and, with the help of Nicodemus, anointed it for burial in an unused tomb. (Only the wealthy could afford to acquire such sepulchers.)

Joseph of Arimathea, being a disciple of Jesus, but a secret one for fear of the Jews, asked Pilate that he might take away the body of Jesus; and Pilate granted permission. So he came and took away His body. Nicodemus, who had first come to Him by night, also came, bringing a mixture of myrrh and aloes, about a hundred pounds weight. So they took the body of Jesus and bound it in linen wrappings with the spices, as is the burial custom of the Jews. Now in the place where He was crucified there was a garden, and in the garden a new tomb in which no one had yet been laid. Therefore because of the Jewish day of preparation, since the tomb was nearby, they laid Jesus there.   (John 19:38–42)

Joseph of Arimathea, a prominent member of the Council, who was himself waiting for the kingdom of God, went boldly to Pilate and asked for Jesus' body. Pilate was surprised to hear that he was already dead. Summoning the centurion, he asked him if Jesus had already died. When he learned from the centurion that it was so, he gave the body to Joseph. So Joseph bought some linen cloth, took down the body, wrapped it in the linen, and placed it in a tomb cut out of rock. Then he rolled a stone against the entrance of the tomb.   (Mark 15:43–46 NIV)

Joseph of Arimathea's actions fulfilled these prophetic words of Isaiah:

He was assigned a grave with the wicked, and with the rich in his death, though he had done no violence, nor was any deceit in his mouth.

(Isaiah 53:9 NIV)

Not Abandoned to Sheol

To the Hebrews, the name *Sheol,* or *Hades,* referred to the destination of a person's soul after death, while his or her earthly body decayed in its grave. Sheol was known as the "underworld," a place of no return.

David composed a psalm that proved to be prophetic about how Jesus' body would not stay in the grave, nor would His soul stay in the underworld:

My flesh also will dwell securely. For You will not abandon my soul to Sheol; nor will You allow Your Holy One to undergo decay.

(Psalm 16:9–10)

This psalm was not about David, who died in the usual way and whose body remained buried. Rather, his words applied directly to "the fruit of his body"—one of his descendants, Jesus Christ. Peter stated,

Brethren, I may confidently say to you regarding the patriarch David that he both died and was buried, and his tomb is with us to this day. And so, because he was a prophet and knew that God had sworn to him with an oath to seat one of his descendants on his throne, he looked ahead and spoke of the resurrection of the Christ, that He was neither abandoned to Hades, nor did His flesh suffer decay. This Jesus God raised up again, to which we are all witnesses.   (Acts 2:29–32)

He Bore the Sin of Many

The prophecies and their fulfillments roll on. Although Isaiah had never met someone who could erase the wickedness of sin, he prophesied about such a One:

> I will divide Him a portion with the great, and He shall divide the spoil with the strong, because He poured out His soul unto death, and He was numbered with the transgressors, and He bore the sin of many, and made intercession for the transgressors. (Isaiah 53:12 NKJV)

Soon after Jesus' resurrection, His disciples began to understand what He had done, that He had completed the most improbable accomplishment that the ancient prophecies had predicted—the reconciliation of humankind with God.

> Then He [Jesus, talking with two of His disciples on the road to Emmaus] opened their minds to understand the Scriptures, and He said to them, "Thus it is written, that the Christ would suffer and rise again from the dead the third day, and that repentance for forgiveness of sins would be proclaimed in His name to all the nations, beginning from Jerusalem." (Luke 24:45–47)

> [God] made Him who knew no sin to be sin on our behalf, so that we might become the righteousness of God in Him.
> (2 Corinthians 5:21)

> For if by the transgression of the one the many died, much more did the grace of God and the gift by the grace of the one Man, Jesus Christ, abound to the many. (Romans 5:15)

On one of my prayer journeys to Israel, I had the delight of walking on the ancient road to Emmaus. It is not a popular tourist site. It is uncared-for and overtaken with weeds. But this was the road on which the resurrected Christ joined two of His disciples who, in their discouraged condition, failed to recognize Him, even as their hearts burned strangely when He opened the Scriptures to them. (See Luke 24:13–32.)

That day, my heart burned within as our little group of prayerful pilgrims paused to read from Luke 24, putting ourselves into the sandals of those two despondent disciples. The eyes of the heart (see Ephesians 1:18) of these disciples did not stay closed. They were opened and enlightened!

How about you? Does your heart burn warmly within for the Messiah, the Son of God? Do you need the eyes of your heart to be opened? Then pause right now. Admit your need and ask Jesus to do for you what He did for the disciples on the road to Emmaus.

Does your heart burn warmly within for the Messiah,
the Son of God?

A New Covenant Foretold

Before the Messiah came, the Jews lived strictly under the covenants that had been established by God with Noah, Abraham, and Moses. They hoped that someday a Messiah would arrive on the scene, and that somehow this advent would usher in a new covenant that would enfold and complete all previous ones. But I am sure that even the most dedicated scholar of the Scriptures could not have anticipated how that new covenant would come about. Even now, it's almost too much to wrap one's mind around. The following is a quick "covenant history lesson."

The First Blood Sacrifice

After God had created Adam and Eve, the only commandment He gave them was not to eat any fruit from the tree of the knowledge of good and evil. The penalty for disobedience would be death. (See Genesis 2:16–17.) Sadly, as we know, they did disobey, which is to say that they sinned, and God cast them out of His presence. Before He did so, however, He covered their shame and nakedness by making them garments from animal skin. (See Genesis 3:6–24.)

In order to make these garments, God had to cause the first death of an animal, which means that an animal had to die—its blood had to be shed—because of human sin. This was a prototype of the blood sacrifices for sin that God would later institute with His chosen people.

The First Covenant—Noah and the Flood

After the fall of humankind, things on earth went from bad to worse. Wickedness characterized the human race, and God decided to take drastic action. He told the one righteous man, Noah, to build a huge boat, in which he could preserve his own family line and salvage enough animals to repopulate the world after a flood of unprecedented proportions. Noah not only obeyed, but he also voluntarily made a sacrifice of thanksgiving when it was over.

> Then Noah built an altar to the LORD, and took of every clean animal and of every clean bird and offered burnt offerings on the altar. The LORD smelled the soothing aroma; and the LORD said to Himself, "I will never again curse the ground on account of man, for the intent of man's heart is evil from his youth; and I will never again destroy every living thing, as I have done...." [The Lord said to Noah,] "I establish My covenant with you; and all flesh shall never again be cut off by the water of the flood, neither shall there again be a flood to destroy the earth....I set My bow in the cloud, and it shall be for a sign of a covenant between Me and the earth. It shall come about, when I bring a cloud over the earth, that the bow will be seen in the cloud, and I will remember My covenant, which is between Me and you and every living creature of all flesh; and never again shall the water become a flood to destroy all flesh." (Genesis 8:20–21; 9:11, 13–15)

The Scripture says that God smelled the soothing aroma of the roasting animal flesh. After He "breathed" it in, He "exhaled" a covenant of blessing and protection, which He has honored to this day. (A covenant is a sovereign promise of blessing that is most binding when it is based on a blood sacrifice.)

The Second Covenant—the Abrahamic Promise

God's promise to Noah became part of the teachings of the people who carried on and developed the worship of the one true God. Eventually, a man named Abram came along, and God selected him to become the father of countless descendants, all of whom could benefit from a fresh covenant that God decreed to Abram (whom He later renamed Abraham):

> *I will bless those who bless you, and the one who curses you I will curse. And in you all the families of the earth will be blessed.* (Genesis 12:3)

> *I will establish My covenant between Me and you and your descendants after you in their generations, for an everlasting covenant, to be God to you and your descendants after you. Also I give to you and your descendants after you the land in which you are a stranger, all the land of Canaan, as an everlasting possession; and I will be their God....As for you, you shall keep My covenant, you and your descendants after you throughout their generations. This is My covenant which you shall keep, between Me and you and your descendants after you: Every male child among you shall be circumcised.*   (Genesis 17:7–10 NKJV)

The Third Covenant—the Sinai Covenant

These earlier covenants were meant to lead up to a third covenant, obtained by Moses on Mount Horeb (Sinai), sealed and reconfirmed for generations afterward by animal blood sacrifices in the temple.

> *The LORD our God made a covenant with us at Horeb. The LORD did not make this covenant with our fathers, but with us, with all those of us alive here today.*   (Deuteronomy 5:2–3)

> *Then [Moses] sent young men of the children of Israel, who offered burnt offerings and sacrificed peace offerings of oxen to the LORD. And Moses took half the blood and put it in basins, and half the blood he sprinkled on the altar. Then he took the Book of the Covenant and read in the hearing of the people. And they said, "All that the LORD has said we will do, and be obedient." And Moses took the blood, sprinkled it on the people, and said, "This is the blood of the covenant which the LORD has made with you according to all these words."*
> (Exodus 24:5–8 NKJV)

In my view, the words of the people are a good statement of faith for us today. We could repeat them often: *"All that the LORD has said we will do, and be obedient."*

The Messiah Fulfills the New Covenant

Well before Jesus came, the prophets were stirring with news of a "new covenant" that would be better than all the previous ones. This new covenant would not supersede the old ones as much as it would fulfill them, translating what sufficed as only a temporary, repeated covering for sin into a permanent sin-remover. Jeremiah recorded the word of the Lord regarding this new covenant:

> *Behold, the days are coming, says the LORD, when I will make a new covenant with the house of Israel and with the house of Judah—not according to the covenant that I made with their fathers in the day that I took them by the hand to lead them out of the land of Egypt, My covenant which they broke, though I was a husband to them, says the LORD. But this is the covenant that I will make with the house of Israel after those days, says the LORD: I will put My law in their minds, and write it on their hearts; and I will be their God, and they shall be My people. No more shall every man teach his neighbor, and every man his brother, saying, "Know the LORD," for they all shall know Me, from the least of them to the greatest of them, says the LORD. For I will forgive their iniquity, and their sin I will remember no more.*
> (Jeremiah 31:31–34 NKJV)

One of the Hebrew words translated as *"new"* (used in *"**new** covenant,"* above) is *chadash,* which means a "fresh, new thing." This word is also found in a number of other Old Testament Scriptures, such as the following:

> *Behold, the former things have come to pass, now I declare new things; before they spring forth I proclaim them to you.*   (Isaiah 42:9)

> *I will give them one heart, and put a new spirit within them. And I will take the heart of stone out of their flesh and give them a heart of*

flesh, that they may walk in My statutes and keep My ordinances and do them. Then they will be My people, and I shall be their God.

(Ezekiel 11:19–20)

I will sprinkle clean water on you, and you will be clean; I will cleanse you from all your filthiness and from all your idols. Moreover, I will give you a new heart and put a new spirit within you; and I will remove the heart of stone from your flesh and give you a heart of flesh. I will put My Spirit within you and cause you to walk in My statutes, and you will be careful to observe My ordinances.   (Ezekiel 36:25–27)

Jesus Christ made all these promises real by establishing a brand-new covenant, using His own blood instead of the blood of a lamb or of another animal. This new covenant is like the "heart transplant" that Ezekiel talked about. The newer part of our Bible is known as the New Testament, or new covenant, because everything centers on what Jesus did. New Testament writers were very clear about this.

God was in Christ reconciling the world to Himself, not counting their trespasses against them, and He has committed to us the word of reconciliation.….He made Him who knew no sin to be sin on our behalf, so that we might become the righteousness of God in Him.

(2 Corinthians 5:19, 21)

[Christ] is the head of the body, the church, who is the beginning, the firstborn from the dead, that in all things He may have the preeminence. For it pleased the Father that in Him all the fullness should dwell, and by Him to reconcile all things to Himself, by Him, whether things on earth or things in heaven, having made peace through the blood of His cross. And you, who once were alienated and enemies in your mind by wicked works, yet now He has reconciled in the body of His flesh through death, to present you holy, and blameless, and above reproach in His sight.   (Colossians 1:18–22 NKJV)

Now may the God of peace who brought up our Lord Jesus from the dead, that great Shepherd of the sheep, through the blood of the

everlasting covenant, make you complete in every good work to do
His will, working in you what is well pleasing in His sight, through
Jesus Christ, to whom be glory forever and ever. Amen.
(Hebrews 13:20–21 NKJV)

"What can wash away my sin? Nothing but the blood of Jesus."[11] The precious blood of the Lamb of God was shed for all humankind, once and for all.

Jesus Christ, King Messiah

King Messiah Is the Son of David

At last! Now the disciples and others knew that the Suffering Servant of prophecy was the same as the Messiah and King of prophecy, and that Jesus Christ had truly accomplished what the prophets could only hint at. They had always known that the Messiah had something to do with King David, but in the intervening years, David's lineage had expanded and dispersed. Who would have expected the Messiah to slip into view with so little fanfare?

My covenant I will not violate, nor will I alter the utterance of My lips.
Once I have sworn by My holiness; I will not lie to David. His descen-
dants shall endure forever and his throne as the sun before Me.
(Psalm 89:34–36)

When your days are over and you [David] rest with your ancestors, I
will raise up your offspring to succeed you, your own flesh and blood,
and I will establish his kingdom. He is the one who will build a house
for my Name, and I will establish the throne of his kingdom forever. I
will be his father, and he will be my son....Your house and your king-
dom will endure forever before me; your throne will be established for-
ever.
(2 Samuel 7:12–14, 16 NIV)

---

11. Robert Lowry, "Nothing but the Blood" (alternate title "What Can Wash Away My Sin?"), 1876.

And [Isaiah] said, Hear then, O house of David! Is it a small thing for you to weary and try the patience of men, but will you weary and try the patience of my God also? Therefore the Lord Himself shall give you a sign: Behold, the young woman who is unmarried and a virgin shall conceive and bear a son, and shall call his name Immanuel [God with us]. (Isaiah 7:13–14 AMP)

When [Bartimaeus] heard that it was Jesus of Nazareth, he began to shout, "Jesus, Son of David, have mercy on me!" Many rebuked him and told him to be quiet, but he shouted all the more, "Son of David, have mercy on me!" (Mark 10:47–48 NIV)

In case you have ever wondered why Matthew started his gospel with that lengthy genealogy, it was to show that Jesus Christ the Man did in fact descend from King David. (See Matthew 1, especially verses 1 and 6.) Isn't the Bible breathtaking? Not one line is wasted.

King Messiah Is Not a Mere Man

Why would blind Bartimaeus cry out *"Son of David"* instead of "Son of God" or "Son of Man"? It's because he, along with much of the rest of the population in Israel, had the prophecies drilled into his consciousness. The people of Israel were anticipating the fulfillment of the Word, right down to the last detail. They knew that Messiah would be a descendant of King David. What they didn't know was that He would be far more than a mere mortal—He would be fully God *and* fully Man. The fact that He would be God Himself had been prophesied but not fully understood:

I beheld till the thrones were cast down, and the Ancient of days did sit, whose garment was white as snow, and the hair of his head like the pure wool: his throne was like the fiery flame, and his wheels as burning fire. A fiery stream issued and came forth from before him: thousand thousands ministered unto him, and ten thousand times ten thousand stood before him: the judgment was set, and the books were opened.... I saw in the night visions, and, behold, one like the Son of man came with the clouds of heaven, and came to the Ancient of days, and they brought him near before him. And there was given him dominion, and

*glory, and a kingdom, that all people, nations, and languages, should
serve him: his dominion is an everlasting dominion, which shall not
pass away, and his kingdom that which shall not be destroyed.*

(Daniel 7:9–10, 13–14 KJV)

*I set my king upon my holy hill of Zion. I will declare the decree: the
LORD hath said unto me, Thou art my Son; this day have I begotten
thee. Ask of me, and I shall give thee the heathen for thine inheritance,
and the uttermost parts of the earth for thy possession. Thou shalt break
them with a rod of iron; thou shalt dash them in pieces like a potter's
vessel. Be wise now therefore, O ye kings: be instructed, ye judges of the
earth.*

(Psalm 2:6–10 KJV)

What Daniel saw in his vision was unprecedented—the suffering
Messiah and the reigning King would be one and the same. His first advent
would lead to His second advent, at which time He would be handed an
everlasting dominion that would never disappear. All peoples, nations, and
languages would serve the Son of God, Jesus the Christ.

---

*What Daniel saw in his vision was unprecedented—the suffering
Messiah and the reigning King would be one and the same.*

And when the Man Jesus stood before the high priest, Caiaphas, on
trial for His life, He could not have been clearer about His equally important identity as the Son of God:

*The high priest said to Him, "I adjure You by the living God, that You
tell us whether You are the Christ, the Son of God." Jesus said to him,
"You have said it yourself; nevertheless I tell you, hereafter you will see
the Son of Man sitting at the right hand of Power, and coming on the
clouds of heaven." Then the high priest tore his robes and said, "He has
blasphemed! What further need do we have of witnesses? Behold, you
have now heard the blasphemy; what do you think?" They answered,
"He deserves death!"*

(Matthew 26:63–66)

They sent Him off to be crucified, thinking that by killing Him, they would eliminate a blasphemous false messiah. They were grievously mistaken. Not only did Jesus, the true Messiah, rise from the grave and establish His kingdom in the hearts of people everywhere, but He will in fact come again in absolute authority as a conquering King. He is King Messiah, described by John in Revelation as follows:

> I saw heaven opened, and behold, a white horse, and He who sat on it is called Faithful and True, and in righteousness He judges and wages war. His eyes are a flame of fire, and on His head are many diadems; and He has a name written on Him which no one knows except Himself. He is clothed with a robe dipped in blood, and His name is called The Word of God. And the armies which are in heaven, clothed in fine linen, white and clean, were following Him on white horses. From His mouth comes a sharp sword, so that with it He may strike down the nations, and He will rule them with a rod of iron; and He treads the wine press of the fierce wrath of God, the Almighty. And on His robe and on His thigh He has a name written, "KING OF KINGS, AND LORD OF LORDS." (Revelation 19:11–16)

When He comes that time, the One who already fulfilled so many prophecies in His first advent will fulfill the rest of the words recorded in Scripture about Him that are awaiting realization. This is why we say, with the whole church, in all times and places, *"Even so, come, Lord Jesus!"* (Revelation 22:20 NKJV).

Jesus Christ, Messiah, Son of God and Son of Man, King of all kings and Lord of all lords—come quickly! For the glory of God the Father, amen.

6

The Person of the Holy Spirit

Through my study of the Greek New Testament,
I have come to the conclusion that the presence or absence of
the in conjunction with the Holy Spirit marks an important
distinction. When Holy Spirit is not preceded by the,
it denotes something nonpersonal—life, or a power, a force,
a presence, an influence. When Holy Spirit is preceded by the,
on the other hand, He is being depicted as a Person.[12]
—Derek Prince

When I was driving my car one day, I started thinking about the Holy Spirit. I was wondering why, since He is the third Person of the Trinity and just as fully God as the Father and the Son, He gets so much less attention than They. The Apostles' Creed barely mentions Him. His name is always tagged on last: Father, Son, and Holy Spirit. Even believers who call themselves "Spirit-filled" seem to find Him the most difficult member of the Trinity to talk about. To many, He seems mysterious and elusive, like a ghost. And yet, the Holy Spirit proves to be indispensable to our personal conversion, our growth in Christ, and the ongoing building of God's glorious kingdom on the earth. So, why are we so vague about Him?

12. Derek Prince, *Transformed for Life* (Grand Rapids, MI: Chosen Books, 2002), 63.

The insight that I came up with is not a deep theological truth. But here's what hit me: The Holy Spirit is always on the move! Therefore, when we try to "pin Him down," we can't. He has already moved somewhere else. The very first mention of the Spirit of God is in the first chapter of the Bible. And what is He doing? He is moving:

> *In the beginning God created the heavens and the earth. The earth was formless and void, and darkness was over the surface of the deep, and the Spirit of God was moving over the surface of the waters.*
>
> (Genesis 1:1–2)

Another reason the Spirit gets overlooked is quite simply because He does not draw attention to Himself. His work is to exalt the Lord Jesus Christ and to instruct His followers to do the same. (See John 16:14.)

I don't want to overlook Him or "relegate" Him to the periphery. With His help, I want to tell you what He is like. If you have not already gotten to know the Holy Spirit, you can consider this chapter your introduction to your personal Guide and Comforter.

The "Executive Power" Behind the Scenes

As I said above, the Holy Spirit is always moving. He is always active, even when the only evidence of His presence is something like a breeze, a *"whoosh."* As Jesus told Nicodemus, *"The wind blows where it wishes and you hear the sound of it, but do not know where it comes from and where it is going; so is everyone who is born of the Spirit"* (John 3:8). You cannot see the wind, but you can feel the wind, hear the wind, observe the effects of the wind, and channel the wind into useful purpose. It is similar with the Holy Spirit. He makes us "wind-driven" believers!

Andrew Murray, a South African pastor-teacher who wrote more than two hundred books about the Christian life, many of which have remained in print for over a hundred years, defined the Holy Spirit in this way:

> The Father is the eternal being—I Am—the hidden foundation of all things and fountain of all life. The Son is the outward form, the express image, the revelation of God. The Spirit is the executive

power of the Godhead, creating effect or result. The nature of the hidden unity is revealed and made known in the Son, and that is imparted to us and is experienced by us through the agency of the Spirit.[13]

The Holy Spirit is always executing and revealing things; that is His nature. This is why Jesus said,

> When He, the Spirit of truth, comes, He will guide you into all the truth; for He will not speak on His own initiative, but whatever He hears, He will speak; and He will disclose to you what is to come. He will glorify Me, for He will take of Mine and will disclose it to you. All things that the Father has are Mine; therefore I said that He takes of Mine and will disclose it to you.　　　　　(John 16:13–15)

This is the reason Jesus urged His disciples and other followers to wait for the Spirit to come, saying, "You will receive power when the Holy Spirit has come upon you" (Acts 1:8). They never got very far without the Holy Spirit, and neither will we. I, for one, cannot imagine living the Christian life without the empowering work of the Holy Spirit—being dependent upon His every move, whisper, and nudge.

The Spirit is always in motion, but not because He's restless. He is always working because He has so much to do. He is always moving over the face of the earth to meet the needs of this groaning planet. He is always introducing people to Jesus and teaching them to glorify Jesus, who in turn glorifies the Father.

Wherever the Holy Spirit lands, and wherever people cooperate with Him, things change. Soon, even the atmosphere of the place is different, because the presence of God dwells there. You can tell when this is the case. People start loving Jesus—thanks entirely to the Holy Spirit's behind-the-scenes activity. They love Jesus, and they love the Bible, more than before.

It is so refreshing when believers make room for powerful, life-changing experiences that occur in a Spirit-infused environment. When the members of a church desire the moving of the Dove of God more than they love their own programs and agendas, they experience greater

13. Andrew Murray, *The Blood of Christ* (Bloomington, MN: Bethany House, 2001), 234.

joy, greater power, and greater hope. They obtain divine direction and the grace to follow God.

I love the Holy Spirit! I want to honor Him as God, yield to Him, and learn to cooperate with Him in His every move.

It is so refreshing when believers make room for powerful, life-changing experiences that occur in a Spirit-infused environment.

The Holy Spirit Is a Person

Some people say that the Spirit is an "influence," but they don't go far enough. He is a Person, Someone with a mind, a will, and emotions, just like the Father and the Son. The following is a foundational definition of the third Person of the Trinity:

> The Holy Spirit is the third divine person of the eternal Godhead, co-equal, co-eternal, and co-existent with the Father and the Son. It is His ministry to convict and convert man as well as to reveal the Son and the Father to the believer. Since the glorification of the Lord Jesus Christ, the Holy Spirit in all His glorious operations is working through all who believe on the Father through the Son.[14]

The Holy Spirit brings people to new birth in Christ and dwells within them, providing all kinds of help as they learn to navigate their new life. Before His ascension to heaven, Jesus explained to His disciples that, although He Himself would no longer be walking and talking with His followers, He would send His Spirit to pick up where He had left off. (See John 16:5–16.) They found it hard to believe that anything could improve upon the resurrected presence of the Master. Yet Jesus said, *"It is to your advantage that I go away; for if I do not go away, the Helper will not come to you; but if I go, I will send Him to you"* (John 16:7). Jesus did send His Spirit (see Acts 2), and His Spirit is still with us to this day.

---

14. Kevin J. Conner, *The Foundations of Christian Doctrine* (Portland, OR: City Bible Publishing, 1980), 71.

The Role of the Holy Spirit

How could be it to our advantage to have the Spirit instead of Jesus Himself? What kinds of things should we expect Him to do? I will inevitably leave something out, but here are the main facts about the Holy Spirit and His role that we can find in the scriptural accounts of His comings and goings:

1. He will guide us. Jesus promised,

> *When He, the Spirit of truth, has come, He will guide you into all truth; for He will not speak on His own authority, but whatever He hears He will speak; and He will tell you things to come. He will glorify Me, for He will take of what is Mine and declare it to you.*
>
> (John 16:13–14 NKJV)

2. He will speak to us, just as He spoke to Philip: *"Then the Spirit said to Philip, 'Go up and join this chariot'"* (Acts 8:29). Often, His words are few, but He always says exactly what is most needed.

3. He can strive and contend with ungodliness. In the time of Noah, as wickedness increased across the face of the earth, *"the LORD said, "My Spirit shall not strive with man forever, for he is indeed flesh"* (Genesis 6:3 NKJV).

4. He can be lied to. It's not a good idea to do it, though! A married couple in the early church found this out the hard way. *"Then Peter said, 'Ananias, how is it that Satan has so filled your heart that you have lied to the Holy Spirit and have kept for yourself some of the money you received for the land?'"* (Acts 5:3 NIV).

5. He can be grieved. We know this is the case, because Paul warned the people of Ephesus not to grieve Him: *"Do not grieve the Holy Spirit of God, by whom you were sealed for the day of redemption"* (Ephesians 4:30). One of the primary ways in which He can be grieved is by our detrimental speech.

6. He can be sinned against. Again, such an action can have dire repercussions: *"Whoever blasphemes against the Holy Spirit will never be forgiven; they are guilty of an eternal sin"* (Mark 3:29 NIV). This is not popular teaching today—but these are the words of our Master Jesus.

7. He searches all things, and He reveals the things of God to us.

God has revealed them [the things God has prepared for those who love Him] *to us through His Spirit. For the Spirit searches all things, yes, the deep things of God. For what man knows the things of a man except the spirit of the man which is in him? Even so no one knows the things of God except the Spirit of God.* (1 Corinthians 2:10–11 NKJV)

8. He makes intercession for us. *"Likewise the Spirit also helps in our weaknesses. For we do not know what we should pray for as we ought, but the Spirit Himself makes intercession for us with groanings which cannot be uttered"* (Romans 8:26 NKJV). I can certainly relate to this aspect of the Holy Spirit's ministry. Often, I have found myself up against a wall, not knowing what to do or even how to pray. Apart from the Holy Spirit, I am unable to express to God what I and others really need. So, I lean into Him and ask for His help in this thing called prayer. He always proves to be my Helper.

9. He distributes gifts. *"Now there are varieties of gifts, but the same Spirit....But one and the same Spirit works all these things, distributing* [a gift or gifts] *to each one individually just as He wills"* (1 Corinthians 12:4, 11). In this same chapter, some of the gifts of the Spirit are listed in detail. (See 1 Corinthians 12:8–10, 28.)

I love giving gifts. Just ask my kids! It is one of my great joys. Perhaps I am emulating, in part, this quality of the Holy Spirit, who loves to give good gifts to the Father's kids—gifts that heal, gifts that encourage, gifts that empower.

10. He is referred to as Counselor, Comforter, Helper, Advocate, and more. Jesus said:

The Advocate, the Holy Spirit, whom the Father will send in my name, will teach you all things and will remind you of everything I have said to you. (John 14:26 NIV)

When the Comforter (Counselor, Helper, Advocate, Intercessor, Strengthener, Standby) comes, Whom I will send to you from the Father, the Spirit of Truth Who comes (proceeds) from the Father, He [Himself] will testify regarding Me. (John 15:26 AMP)

The best part of having the Holy Spirit as Counselor, Comforter, and Helper is that He *listens*. He does not interrupt. He hears our hearts, and He responds to our invitations with the perfect word or action. When I teach my God Encounters classes, I often conduct a survey in which I ask my students what the Holy Spirit does. I always get great answers. But this one thing people almost always overlook: the fact that the Holy Spirit listens! Besides listening to us, He listens to heaven. He never speaks on His own initiative, but He speaks only what He hears the Father and the Son saying.

When we lean into the Spirit's presence, we can listen to what He is listening to—the very heart of God. It's all about relationship. This is not a set of rules or routines. It is a living, personal relationship through and through.

The Deity of the Holy Spirit

Sometimes, we have a problem remembering that the Holy Spirit is God, although it's not because we think of Him as more human than Godlike (as we might think of Jesus) or as so remote and intimidating that we can't relate to Him (as we might think of the Father). But we can have the tendency to disregard His deity, thinking of Him as something "other" than God, not quite the same as God.

It's easy for us to skim over the direct statements in Scripture that say the Holy Spirit is God, not realizing what we are reading. For example, in the story about Ananias and Sapphira, we usually pay more attention to the shocking events that transpired than to this statement from Peter, which we looked at previously:

> *Ananias, why has Satan filled your heart to lie to the Holy Spirit…?…Why have you conceived this thing in your heart? You have not lied to men but to God.* (Acts 5:3–4 NKJV)

Remember, the Holy Spirit believes He is the Lord God—and He is:

> *Now the Lord is the Spirit, and where the Spirit of the Lord is, there is liberty. But we all, with unveiled face, beholding as in a mirror the*

glory of the Lord, are being transformed into the same image from
glory to glory, just as from the Lord, the Spirit.

(2 Corinthians 3:17–18)

The following verse clearly equates the Holy Spirit with God by referring to Him as *"the Spirit of God"*: *"Do you not know that you are a temple of*
God and that the Spirit of God dwells in you?" (1 Corinthians 3:16).

Of course, we should realize that the Holy Spirit is God, because we
know He is eternal and omnipresent. (See Hebrews 9:14; Psalm 139:7.) In
addition, key "God" titles apply to Him, such as Spirit of Life and Spirit of
Truth. (See, for example, Romans 8:2; John 16:13.) As I mentioned earlier, He is named as an active divine participant in Creation. (See Genesis
1:2.) The Spirit acts just like God. He is also the One who makes our re-
birth and regeneration happen. (See, for example, Titus 3:5.) Again, when
Jesus explained to Nicodemus the necessity of being born again, He ended
by saying, *"The wind blows wherever it pleases. You hear its sound, but you*
cannot tell where it comes from or where it is going. So it is with everyone born
of the Spirit" (John 3:8 NIV). And, after His crucifixion, Jesus was raised
from the dead *"through"* or *"by"* the Spirit. (See Romans 8:11 NASB, NKJV,
AMP, KJV.)

To sum up the deity of the Holy Spirit, Bible teacher James Montgomery
Boice wrote,

> The personality and deity of the Holy Spirit are practical teach-
> ings, for it is by the activity of this divine being that the gospel of
> salvation in Jesus Christ is made clear to us and changes our lives.
> He is the key to a vital and truly personal religion.[15]

Key "God" titles apply to the Holy Spirit, such as
Spirit of Life and Spirit of Truth.

---

15. James Montgomery Boice, *Foundations of the Christian Faith* (Downers Grove, IL: IVP
Academic, 1986), 379.

Five Great Redemptive Acts

The Holy Spirit was no less present than the Father and the Son at any of the five great junctures in the story of God's redemption of humankind. Let's take a glance at the Spirit's involvement in these important events.

1. The Incarnation of Jesus

By the agency of the Holy Spirit, God the Father incarnated Jesus the Son in the womb of the Virgin Mary:

> *The angel answered and said to* [Mary], *"The Holy Spirit will come upon you, and the power of the Most High will overshadow you; and for that reason the holy Child shall be called the Son of God."*
> (Luke 1:35; see also Matthew 1:20)

2. The Earthly Ministry of Jesus

God the Father anointed Jesus the Son with the power of the Holy Spirit. The result: healing and deliverance for humanity. *"You know of Jesus of Nazareth, how God anointed Him with the Holy Spirit and with power, and how He went about doing good and healing all who were oppressed by the devil, for God was with Him"* (Acts 10:38).

Recall how this anointing transpired. Jesus, the Son of God, submitted to baptism under the hands of a young man named John the Baptist, who was His cousin, not much older than He at the time but not divine. After Jesus had come up from the water, the Holy Spirit descended like a dove to rest on Him. (See Matthew 3:16; Mark 1:10; Luke 3:22.) Then, the Father spoke audibly, *"This is My beloved Son, in whom I am well-pleased"* (Matthew 3:17; see also Mark 1:11; Luke 3:22). In these brief minutes, we see all three Persons of the Trinity: the Father, the Holy Spirit, and, of course, the Son.

3. The Atonement of Jesus

When Jesus offered up His life, He took human sin out of the equation so that we could receive salvation. He offered Himself to God the Father through the Holy Spirit, and His sacrifice was effective, because it was accomplished in the Spirit.

Not with the blood of goats and calves, but with His own blood He entered the Most Holy Place once for all, having obtained eternal redemption....How much more shall the blood of Christ, who through the eternal Spirit offered Himself without spot to God, cleanse your conscience from dead works to serve the living God?

(Hebrews 9:12, 14 NKJV)

4. The Resurrection of Jesus

After Jesus' sacrificial death on the cross, God the Father raised His Son from the dead—by the power of the Holy Spirit. Paul introduced his letter to the church in Rome with words to that effect, speaking of what the good news consists of: "*...concerning His Son Jesus Christ our Lord, who was born of the seed of David according to the flesh, and declared to be the Son of God with power according to the Spirit of holiness, by the resurrection from the dead*" (Romans 1:3–4 NKJV).

5. The Gift of the Holy Spirit

At Pentecost, Jesus the Son received from God the Father the gift of the Holy Spirit, and He distributed the gift upon the heads of His disciples like tongues of flame. (See Acts 2:1–4.) That day, Peter preached to the assembled crowd and said, "*God has raised this Jesus to life, and we are all witnesses of it. Exalted to the right hand of God, he has received from the Father the promised Holy Spirit and has poured out what you now see and hear*" (Acts 2:32–33 NIV). Again, we see the Spirit in conjunction with the Son and the Father.

Likewise, the ongoing relationship of God to His people in this present age directly involves all three Persons of the Godhead. The end purpose of God is that we would come to Him as Father, but we have access to God the Father only through Jesus the Son, by the Holy Spirit: "*In [Christ] you also are being built together into a dwelling of God in the Spirit*" (Ephesians 2:22).

For it is through Him that we both [whether far off or near] now have an introduction (access) by one [Holy] Spirit to the Father [so that we are able to approach Him]. Therefore you are no longer outsiders (exiles, migrants, and aliens, excluded from the rights of citizens), but you now share citizenship with the saints (God's own people, conse-crated and set apart for Himself); and you belong to God's [own] household.   (Ephesians 2:18–19 AMP)

The Continuing Activity of the Holy Spirit

Near the close of His earthly ministry, the resurrected Jesus promised to give His disciples the gift of the Holy Spirit.

Then He said to them, "Thus it is written, and thus it was necessary for the Christ to suffer and to rise from the dead the third day, and that repentance and remission of sins should be preached in His name to all nations, beginning at Jerusalem. And you are witnesses of these things. Behold, I send the Promise of My Father upon you; but tarry in the city of Jerusalem until you are endued with power from on high."
                                        (Luke 24:46–49 NKJV)

The presence of His Spirit would be ongoing. This promise of the Son is also known as the promise (or glory) of the Father. (See Acts 1:4; Romans 6:4.) The Father and the Son would give the Spirit together. The Father gives only the very best, and He had already given His very best in Jesus. Now, He was giving His very best again in the Holy Spirit.

We know this truth, but we often forget it. God gives His very best to us when we are born again and enter into the new creation realities, which can be summed up as *"Christ in you, the hope of glory"* (Colossians 1:27). So, now, not only is Jesus sitting at the Father's right hand in heaven, but Jesus is also inside us; we become a treasure chest of God. He lives in us in a particular way—by the power of the deity of the Holy Spirit. Not only does the Spirit come upon us for special empowering on special occasions by means of special intercession, but He also lives inside us all the time. He is always near. Because the Holy Spirit is omnipresent, He isn't only a tangible, external presence that manifests on earth at certain times, but He is available to us at all times. And we can be filled with God!

Jesus promised to send the Spirit because He, as a Person, would be leaving His followers. He wanted everyone to know that another Person—the Holy Spirit—would be coming to take His place. There was to be an exchange of Persons. John recorded more of what Jesus said about this:

> *If you love Me, keep My commandments. And I will pray the Father, and He will give you another Helper, that He may abide with you forever—the Spirit of truth, whom the world cannot receive, because it neither sees Him nor knows Him; but you know Him, for He dwells with you and will be in you. I will not leave you orphans; I will come to you.* (John 14:15–18 NKJV)

This passage refers to what subsequently happened at Pentecost. Just a little while before Jesus said this to His disciples, He had spoken of His second coming at the close of the age. (See John 14:3.) This was to show that at no point would He leave us on our own. Never has, never will.

The main purposes of the Holy Spirit on earth are to complete the ministry of Christ and to form the corporate body of Christ, at the same time preparing the bride of Christ (the church) for her Bridegroom, Jesus. (See, for example, John 14:25–26; 16:12–15; Ephesians 2:22; 2 Thessalonians 2:13–14.) The fulfillment of these purposes happens on two levels, the personal and the corporate. Wherever the evil one brings discord, disunity, and disaster, the Spirit works through the body of Christ to generate the kingdom of God.

The "Now Presence," Representing the Godhead

In this age, the Holy Spirit is the resident, personal representative of the Godhead on earth. The dwelling place of this omnipresent Spirit is described in two ways in Scripture—as the physical body (temple) of each believer, and as the church (the collective temple of believers):

> *Do you not know that your bodies are temples of the Holy Spirit, who is in you, whom you have received from God? You are not your own; you were bought at a price. Therefore honor God with your bodies.* (1 Corinthians 6:19–20 NIV)

Don't you know that you yourselves are God's temple and that God's Spirit dwells in your midst? (1 Corinthians 3:16 NIV)

(The *"you"* in verse 16 does not mean you alone, singular; it is plural, and it refers to "you together" as the living temple of God that is the church.)

From His resurrection onward, Jesus has operated in the lives of believers always and only through the Holy Spirit. The scriptural phrasing regarding this fact has become familiar to us, so that we often miss it. Read these passages again with the Spirit in mind:

We were buried therefore with Him by the baptism into death, so that just as Christ was raised from the dead by the glorious [power] of the Father, so we too might [habitually] live and behave in newness of life. (Romans 6:4 AMP)

But if Christ is in you, then even though your body is subject to death because of sin, the Spirit gives life because of righteousness. And if the Spirit of him who raised Jesus from the dead is living in you, he who raised Christ from the dead will also give life to your mortal bodies because of his Spirit who lives in you. (Romans 8:10–11 NIV)

In my former book, Theophilus, I wrote about all that Jesus began to do and to teach until the day he was taken up to heaven, after giving instructions through the Holy Spirit to the apostles he had chosen. (Acts 1:1–2 NIV)

In order to live the Christian life, we need to be just as dependent on the Holy Spirit as Jesus was—and as the early church was. This is why exhortations from Paul such as the following still ring so true for us today:

For those who are led by the Spirit of God are the children of God. The Spirit you received does not make you slaves, so that you live in fear again; rather, the Spirit you received brought about your adoption to sonship. And by him we cry, "Abba, Father." (Romans 8:14–15 NIV)

But if you are led by the Spirit, you are not under the Law.

(Galatians 5:18)

For the Spirit God gave us does not make us timid, but gives us power, love and self-discipline. (2 Timothy 1:7 NIV)

If Jesus did only what He saw His Father doing (see John 5:19), how much more should we be operating from a position of Abba-dependency, through the agency of His Spirit? "Oh, you foolish Western Christians! Who persuaded you to move from operating by the Spirit to operating according to your own souls? What made you think that your great programs and projects were going to accomplish the work that belongs to the third Person of the Godhead?" (See Galatians 3:1–5.)

From His resurrection onward, Jesus has operated in the lives of believers always and only through the Holy Spirit.

What If the Holy Spirit Were Not Here?

It has often been said that if the Holy Spirit had been removed from the first-century church, 90 percent of what the early believers were doing would have ceased, and only 10 percent would have remained. And, in contrast, if the Holy Spirit were to be removed from today's church, 90 percent of what we do would remain and only 10 percent would cease.

I want us to change that percentage—together. Let's rely upon the third Person of the Godhead and let Him rule in the church today! You see, the overarching purpose of the Holy Spirit in this age is to work with the bride of Christ, the church, so that, together, we can cry out, "Come, Lord Jesus!"

In essence, the Scriptures prophetically proclaim, again and again, "*The Spirit and the bride say, 'Come'*" (Revelation 22:17)! Let's welcome the presence, the conviction, the movement, the gifting, and the personal wisdom and ways of the Holy Spirit into our lives in our generation.

This cry from the worldwide body of Christ to be empowered by the Holy Spirit to do the works of Jesus epitomizes passionate pursuit, not just on a personal level but also on a global, end-time level. Let an unbridled cry arise: "Come again, Holy Spirit!"

7

Holy Spirit,
You Are Welcome Here!

The Holy Spirit has personality, though not a [physical body].
Personality is that which possesses intelligence, feeling, and will.
When one possesses the characteristics, properties,
and qualities of personality, then personality can be attributed to
that being. Personality, when used in reference to divine beings,
cannot be measured by human standards.[16]
—Dick Iverson

Oh, how I love the Holy Spirit! He makes Jesus real! He makes the Father enjoyable! I roll out the red carpet to this precious Dove of God every day. I say, "Holy Spirit, You are welcome here!"

The Holy Spirit is the One who connects us to heaven. Without Him, not even Jesus could have known what the Father wanted Him to say or to do. (See, for example, John 5:19.) How much more do we little earthlings need the same Spirit? If you want to know God, you absolutely *must* get to know the Holy Spirit, who works tirelessly to connect heaven and earth.

This Holy Spirit is described in the Scriptures as the "Spirit of Knowledge," which means that He is the Spirit of knowing and of being

16. Dick Iverson, *The Holy Spirit Today* (Portland, OR: Bible Temple Publishing, 1990), 5.

known. In other words, the Spirit has been given to us to make God known, and to make Him knowable. Father God is approachable, but without the Holy Spirit's help, we tend to be afraid of Him. We are afraid because of our sin. But we can approach God without trepidation when we are in Christ (see Hebrews 4:15–16), having the Holy Spirit as our Helper, because the Spirit is our Comforter, or Paraclete (from the Greek *paráklētos*, "close-beside," and "make a call," like a legal advocate who makes the right judgment call, being close to the situation). The Spirit is our Advocate and Encourager. (See, for example, John 14:16, 26 NIV, AMP; Romans 12:8 NIV; 1 Corinthians 14:3 AMP.)

I took the title "Spirit of Knowledge" from one of Isaiah's prophecies about the coming Messiah. Isaiah noted that He would be filled with the Spirit of God, and the prophet expanded on what kind of Spirit this would be:

> *The Spirit of the* LORD *will rest on Him, the spirit of wisdom and understanding, the spirit of counsel and strength, the spirit of knowledge and the fear of the* LORD. (Isaiah 11:2)

The Holy Spirit had an intimate relationship with the Messiah, Yeshua, during His ministry on earth. Jesus humbled Himself, becoming entirely dependent upon the Holy Spirit in order to do and say only those things that would please the Father. Just think about His life and remember what we have covered in previous chapters. Jesus was conceived and born of the Holy Spirit. The Spirit led Him. The Spirit anointed Him for His ministry at His baptism. Everything Jesus did, from resisting temptation in the wilderness to raising the dead, He did by the guidance and power of the Spirit. He offered Himself as a sacrifice by the Spirit. He was raised from the dead by the power of the Spirit. And, so that His followers could truly follow in His footsteps, Jesus was faithful to send His Spirit to them on the day of Pentecost (and to everyone since that time who has believed in Him, stepping into faith and becoming a child of God).

Because Jesus has bestowed the Holy Spirit on those who believe, we can have the Spirit of Knowledge, the Comforter, the Advocate as close to us as our next breath, and He will help us to know God daily. (See, for example, John 15:26.)

If you want to know God, you absolutely must get to know the Holy Spirit, who works tirelessly to connect heaven and earth.

So Many Wonderful Names

In Isaiah 11:2, quoted above, we see more names for the Holy Spirit listed along with the "Spirit of Knowledge (and the Fear of the Lord)." In that one verse, we also find the title "Spirit of Wisdom and Understanding" (or "Spirit of Wisdom and Revelation"; see Ephesians 1:17), as well as "Spirit of Counsel and Strength." I mentioned already that the Holy Spirit is called the "Paraclete," or "Comforter," "Advocate." He is also the "Gift-Giver," as described in chapter 5 of this book. The Spirit executes the Father's will on earth where we human beings are concerned.

Names are extremely significant. They flesh out the defining characteristics of a person or place, and this proves to be true of the way the many names of God's Spirit make known His distinctive persona. Let's take a look at some additional names or titles that have been given to Him, and examine what they show us about the Holy Spirit.

The Holy Spirit. This name, obviously, is the most prevalent name of all (see, for example, Luke 11:13), "holy" meaning sacred, set apart, and utterly pure.

The Spirit of God. We never want to forget this most basic fact: The Father, the Son, and the Holy Spirit together make up the Godhead. Again, at the Creation, *"the Spirit of God was moving over the surface of the waters"* (Genesis 1:2). And Paul used the term *"Spirit of God"* in his letters to believers. Here are some examples: *"You are not in the flesh but in the Spirit, if indeed the Spirit of God dwells in you"* (Romans 8:9). *"For as many as are led by the Spirit of God, these are sons of God"* (Romans 8:14 NKJV). *"Do you not know that you are a temple of God and that the Spirit of God dwells in you?"* (1 Corinthians 3:16).

The Spirit of Christ. Because the Three are one—Father, Son, and Holy Spirit—the Spirit is sometimes specifically called "the Spirit of

Christ." The apostle Paul used this name in his letter to the Christians in Rome: "*If anyone does not have the Spirit of Christ, he does not belong to Him*" (Romans 8:9).

The Dove of God. This name is one of my personal favorites. The Holy Spirit can be called "the Dove of God" because, as we discussed earlier, He appeared in the form of a dove at Jesus' baptism. Like a dove, He descends onto us; and, if we welcome Him, He stays. He woos us and draws us to the Father. In a certain sense, we could say that He romances us in the love of God. The dove nature of the Spirit displays His gentleness, tenderness, innocence, sensitivity, and peace.

The Spirit of Grace. God's grace, which is free to us, is a magnificent topic. It has been the focus of countless sermons and writings, and the concept of "grace alone" was the foundation stone of the entire Great Reformation five hundred years ago. "The Spirit of Grace" is one of the names of the Holy Spirit (see Hebrews 10:29), and the title Spirit of Grace has been used as the name of many churches.

The Spirit of Burning. (See also the reference to "Fire," below.) "*The Lord has washed away the filth of the daughters of Zion and purged the bloodshed of Jerusalem from her midst, by the spirit of judgment and the spirit of burning*" (Isaiah 4:4). We need a sustained revival that includes the experiential conviction of sin and that brings people into true freedom. Perhaps this is part of the ministry of the Spirit of Burning.

The Spirit of Life. The same Spirit who was present at the genesis of all life is the One who replaces death with life for anyone who accepts God's invitation to new life: "*For the law of the Spirit of life [which is] in Christ Jesus [the law of our new being] has freed me from the law of sin and of death*" (Romans 8:2 AMP).

The Spirit of Glory. Most translations of 1 Peter 4:14 contain the phrase "*the Spirit of glory and of God.*" In other words, the Spirit of Glory is the same as the Spirit of God.

The Spirit of Adoption. This is a name with thrilling implications for every believer. "*For as many as are led by the Spirit of God, these are sons of God. For you did not receive the spirit of bondage again to fear, but you received the Spirit of adoption by whom we cry out, 'Abba,*

Father'" (Romans 8:14–15 NKJV). The Holy Spirit makes sure that we can respond to our Father in heaven like true children.

Fire, Water, Wind. While symbols or metaphors are not actual names, per se, they can be almost synonymous with names in regard to defining something or someone. The Holy Spirit is often associated with *fire* (see, for example, Isaiah 4:4; Matthew 3:11), *water* (see, for example, John 7:38–39; 1 Corinthians 10:1–2; Titus 3:5), and *wind* (see Ezekiel 37:7–10; John 3:8; Acts 2:2–3). In the Scriptures, fire emphasizes the act of purging, sanctifying, purifying, burning out dross. Water satisfies thirst and is essential to life. It also cleanses and refreshes. The Spirit brings us into the flow of the fresh, living water of spiritual life. Wind signifies something that we can feel and hear but not see (although we can see its effects). The wind of the Spirit propels us into forward motion.

Seal, or Pledge. The precious Holy Spirit has been given to us as a pledge or earnest (down payment) of the fullness that is yet to come. We have been sealed with the Holy Spirit—forever, we are God's own children. This makes Him the "Spirit of Promise":

> *In Him you also trusted, after you heard the word of truth, the gospel of your salvation; in whom also, having believed, you were sealed with the Holy Spirit of promise, who is the guarantee of our inheritance until the redemption of the purchased possession, to the praise of His glory.*
> (Ephesians 1:13–14 NKJV)

He will ever be with us. (See, for example, Hebrews 13:5.) God's promises appear throughout His Word, including the promise of the arrival of His Spirit. (See, for example, Joel 2:28–29; Ezekiel 36:27.) Right before the Holy Spirit was given at Pentecost, Jesus referred to Him as *"the promise of My Father"* (Luke 24:49; see also Acts 1:4; Galatians 3:14).

Oil. The "oil" of the Spirit anoints us to perform the Father's will, enabling us to walk in Jesus' footsteps. We have seen that Jesus, too, was anointed by the Spirit of God: *"You know of Jesus of Nazareth, how God anointed Him with the Holy Spirit and with power, and how He went about doing good and healing all who were oppressed by the devil, for God was with Him"* (Acts 10:38). By means of this anointing, the Spirit instructs us better than any classroom teacher. John wrote that *"the anointing you received from him remains in you, and you do not need anyone to teach you. But as his anointing teaches you about all things and as that anointing is real, not counterfeit—just as it has taught you, remain in him"* (1 John 2:27 NIV). That's all you have to remember: "Remain in Him."

Your Relationship with the Holy Spirit

Nobody will ever force you into a relationship with God, not even God Himself, although the Holy Spirit is the One who brings God's righteousness to bear on people. His methods, while persuasive and effective, are never coercive. He is the Helper and Caretaker, not a tyrant or a patrol cop. Most of His endeavors can be characterized by action verbs. He *indwells*, He *fills*, He *frees*, He *equips*, He *transforms*, He *convicts*, He *assures*, He *inspires*, He *guides* and *directs*, He *regenerates*—and He *resurrects*. That's a lot!

Let us now look more specifically at the role of the Holy Spirit in our lives.

The Spirit Convicts People of Sin

It is the work of the Holy Spirit to bring each person into deep personal conviction concerning sin, righteousness, and judgment to prepare him or her for salvation. (See, for example, John 16:8–11; 1 Thessalonians 1:5.) He makes it possible for us to come to a point of personal accountability for our sinfulness, setting aside pride and rebellion and self-justification.

The Spirit Regenerates the Believer in the New Birth

By being born again into God's kingdom, a new believer enters into the most intimate personal communion with God possible. *"He saved us, not on the basis of deeds which we have done in righteousness, but according to His mercy, by the washing of regeneration and renewing by the Holy Spirit"* (Titus 3:5). *"For by one Spirit we were all baptized into one body, whether Jews or Greeks, whether slaves or free, and we were all made to drink of one Spirit"* (1 Corinthians 12:13). (See also John 3:5 and John chapters 15 and 17.)

The Spirit Grants the Believer Assurance of Salvation

Because the new birth is an invisible occurrence, some people often wonder afterward if anything happened to them at all. Even before other undeniable evidence of spiritual life starts to show, the Spirit of God graciously assures people, deep within their spirits, that salvation is indeed theirs. *"The Spirit himself testifies with our spirit that we are God's children"* (Romans 8:16 NIV; see also Ephesians 1:13–14).

By being born again into God's kingdom, we enter into the most intimate personal communion with God possible.

The Spirit Indwells and Fills the Believer

"You know Him because He abides with you and will be in you" (John 14:17; see also 2 Timothy 1:14). The Holy Spirit takes up residence in the new believer, and wonderful changes begin to occur. Yet many Christians never seem to understand that the Spirit lives within them. The apostle Paul asked some believers in Ephesus, *"'Did you receive the Holy Spirit when you believed?' They answered, 'No, we have not even heard that there is a Holy Spirit'"* (Acts 19:2 NIV). Paul proceeded to instruct them about the Spirit, and then he prayed for them to receive Him. Another time, he said bluntly, *"If anyone does not have the Spirit of Christ, he does not belong to Him"* (Romans 8:9). On the day of Pentecost, the faithful believers were filled to overflowing with the Spirit of God: *"They were all filled with the Holy Spirit and began to speak with other tongues, as the Spirit gave them utterance"* (Acts 2:4 NKJV; see also Acts 4:31; Ephesians 5:18). We should pray daily to be filled with the Holy Spirit.

The Spirit Sets the Believer Free

The Holy Spirit delivers us from the bondage and power of sin. He opens up new levels of freedom and puts spiritual maturity within our grasp. The Spirit continues to supply us with more than enough power and direction to break bad habits, deal with issues of generational sin, and address seemingly insurmountable problems. Take some time to read (and pray from!) these promises of your rightful liberty and empowerment in the Spirit: Romans 8:1–2; 12:1–2; Ephesians 1:18–21; 3:16; 4:22–24; Colossians 3:10.

The Spirit Equips the Believer for Effective Ministry

The gift of the Spirit is the gift that keeps on giving; the Holy Spirit keeps "filling the sails" of authentic believers, equipping them with all the abilities and strength they could possibly need to do the work of the kingdom of God.

> To each one is given the manifestation of the Spirit for the common good. For to one is given the word of wisdom through the Spirit, and to another the word of knowledge according to the same Spirit; to another faith by the same Spirit, and to another gifts of healing by the one Spirit, and to another the effecting of miracles, and to another prophecy, and to another the distinguishing of spirits, to another various kinds of tongues, and to another the interpretation of tongues. But one and the same Spirit works all these things, distributing to each one individually just as He wills.
>
> (1 Corinthians 12:7–11; see also Ephesians 4:11–12)

Only through an empowering relationship with God's Spirit can anyone actually activate these amazing spiritual gifts to accomplish the spiritual work of God. We cannot do God's work apart from God's Spirit. It's ridiculous even to try to do His work in our own strength. But if we partner with God, we will get His results. (See, for example, Acts 1:8; Romans 12:3–8; 1 Corinthians 4:7.)

The Spirit Produces the Fruit of Character in the Believer

Whenever the Spirit dwells in someone's heart, godly qualities, such as "love, joy, peace, patience, kindness, goodness, faithfulness, gentleness, [and] self-control" (Galatians 5:22–23), begin to ripen in that person's life. We call these qualities "the fruit of the Spirit." Scripture is loaded with references to the positive, righteous character traits that will mature in a believer who is subject to the beneficial influence of the Holy Spirit. (See, for example, Psalm 92:13–14; Matthew 13:23; John 15:2; Romans 5:3–4; 2 Corinthians 6:6; Philippians 1:11; James 3:17; Colossians 1:10.)

The Spirit Enhances the Believer's Communication with God

True communication must be two-way. The Holy Spirit helps us to express prayers that will be heard in heaven (see, for example, Romans 8:26; Jude 20), and He also whispers to our spirits God's words of assurance, guidance, wisdom, and love. In addition, the Spirit gives us the boost we need in order to worship God wholeheartedly and continually. (See, for example, John 4:23–24; Philippians 3:3.) He inspires spiritual songs. (See 1 Corinthians 14:15; Ephesians 5:18–20; Colossians 3:16.) He keeps the flow of communication going both ways.

The Spirit Guides and Directs the Believer in Life

The Spirit faithfully provides all the wisdom and knowledge we need to live holy, obedient lives that are productive by heaven's standards. *"For all who are being led by the Spirit of God, these are sons of God"* (Romans 8:14; see also John 16:13; Acts 10:19–20; 13:2). Make this your prayer: "Spirit of the living God, fall afresh on me!"[17]

The Spirit Will Quicken the Believer's Body at the Resurrection

In light of everything else the Spirit of God does, the last "life experience" we will have with Him, as spectacular as it will be, will not surprise us:

We will not all sleep, but we will all be changed—in a flash, in the twinkling of an eye, at the last trumpet. For the trumpet will sound, the dead will be raised imperishable, and we will be changed. For the perishable must clothe itself with the imperishable, and the mortal with immortality. (1 Corinthians 15:51–53 NIV)

If the Spirit of him who raised Jesus from the dead is living in you, he who raised Christ from the dead will also give life to your mortal bodies because of his Spirit who lives in you. (Romans 8:11 NIV)

Nobody and nothing can separate us from the loving care of God's Spirit. (See Romans 8:35–39.) He is the One who makes sure that we will

---

17. Daniel Iverson, "Spirit of the Living God," 1926.

reach the final shore with our hearts set steadfastly on God, undeterred by sin or difficult circumstances, even death. After traveling together with the Holy Spirit for a lifetime, we will get to know Him so well that, by journey's end, we will recognize our beloved Jesus instantly. As He welcomes us into His Father's heavenly abode, we will clap our hands and exclaim, "I *know* You!"

Nobody and nothing can separate us from
the loving care of God's Spirit.

The Holy Spirit Prepares the Bride

"Here comes the bride, taah-ta-ta-tah!" Wow! I still remember my own delightful wedding day, watching my beautiful bride come down the aisle to meet me. The picture will always be etched in my memory. In recent years, having marched down the aisle myself to give away my two daughters to their respective husbands, I can now view brides and weddings from different angles.

In one way or another, everything the Holy Spirit does is linked to preparing the bride of Christ (again, this is the global church, of which all believers are a part) for her Bridegroom, Jesus. When He returns to claim His bride, she must be beautifully pure and spotless, well prepared for an eternity with Him. The Holy Spirit's job is to make her (us) ready.

For every other task, the Spirit is typified by impersonal metaphors, such as fire, wind, rain, oil, and so forth. But whenever this role of bride preparation is depicted, it occurs through a story that involves people.

One of the best examples is the story in Genesis 24 of how Isaac acquired his bride, Rebekah. Abraham represents God the Father, Isaac is like Jesus the Son, and Rebekah typifies the bride of Christ, the church. A nameless servant plays an important role, and he represents the Holy Spirit. I can see at least nine ways in which this servant is patterned after the Holy Spirit:

1. The servant ruled over all of Father Abraham's possessions and had been given stewardship over Abraham's inheritance. (See Genesis 24:2.) We can see the parallel with the Holy Spirit and Father God.

2. The servant was given the task of selecting a bride for Abraham's son Isaac. (See verses 2–4.) In a similar way, the Holy Spirit has been sent on a specific mission in regard to the church.

3. The servant traveled to another part of the country, bearing lavish gifts and a special proposal. (See verse 10.) Likewise, the Holy Spirit brings to the church God's gifts and an important invitation.

4. The servant approached Rebekah to set in motion his master's offer. Rebekah's response to the servant was all-important; it determined the destiny of her life. (See verses 12–21.) The same is true of our response to the Spirit's invitation to make Jesus our Lord.

5. As soon as Rebekah accepted the servant's offer and his gifts, she was set apart in a special way. (See verses 22–58.) Similarly, when we receive God's Messenger and the gifts He brings, we are repositioned and adorned, set apart for the Bridegroom.

6. Rebekah and her family provided a dwelling place for the servant and his camels. (See verses 23–25, 31–32.) Likewise, the Holy Spirit dwells with the church (the bride-family).

7. The servant became Rebekah's guide to take her to her bridegroom. (See verses 59–61.) This parallels the way the Holy Spirit guides the church to her promised destination and union with Christ.

8. Note that the servant was Rebekah's only source of information about both Abraham and Isaac—types of the Father and the Son. (See verses 34–38.) We, too, must trust the Spirit unequivocally to guide us into all truth.

9. Once the servant had delivered Rebekah to Isaac and Abraham, his task was complete. (See verses 62–67.) He was content to have

accomplished what Abraham had charged him with; he never asked anything for himself. How like the Holy Spirit that was!

Like a seasoned, completely trusted servant, God's Holy Spirit does it all—not only once but continuously, for each individual believer and, consequently, for the corporate body (bride) of Christ. We would be so lost without Him! Without the Spirit, we would never be able to find our way to Jesus, the ultimate Bridegroom.

Honor Him, Seek Him, Give to Him

The Holy Spirit is God, and we should honor Him fully, especially because, as Jesus said, *"when He, the Spirit of truth, comes, He will guide you into all the truth; for He will not speak on His own initiative, but whatever He hears, He will speak; and He will disclose to you what is to come"* (John 16:13). Only by the gentle and powerful ministrations of the Holy Spirit can we know God's truth.

You don't have to wait until something happens spiritually before responding to the Holy Spirit. It is OK to seek Him out in order to instigate action. He likes it when you pursue Him. (Think of the way Jesus responded to the centurion in Luke 7:1–10.) God loves passionate pursuers!

Give the Holy Spirit the freedom and liberty to give *you* freedom and liberty. *"Now the Lord is the Spirit, and where the Spirit of the Lord is, there is liberty (emancipation from bondage, freedom)"* (2 Corinthians 3:17 AMP).

The often-quiet Holy Spirit is not a retiring Spirit—He is an activist. He is the dynamic power that Jesus promised to the church before Pentecost. He executes the purposes and plans of the Godhead. As the One who carries out God's purposes—His creativity, inspiration, conviction, regeneration, generosity, enlightenment, sanctification, and much more—He is always working. (See John 5:17.) Simply by paying attention to what He is doing and by cooperating with Him, we come to understand God better.

Welcome the Holy Spirit right now into your life, your family, your ministry, and your city. Expect great things as you declare, like young Evan

Roberts of the fabled Welsh revival did, "Send the Spirit now, for Jesus Christ's sake."

You know Him well enough by now; with God's Spirit on your side, something good is about to happen.

SECTION TWO

Knowing God by Knowing His Word

Iopen up chapter 8 with this summary statement: "If you want to know God's heart, then you must know His Word, where His nature and character are revealed. The Word speaks to you directly with His voice. I love the God of the Word—and I also love the Word of God!" God is a Master Builder, and He builds upon His Word. In order to know God, you must know His words, as revealed in the Scriptures. They are the foundation of a successful life. Christ, *the* Word of God, is the Cornerstone of that foundation. The wise ones have built their houses upon the rock rather than upon the sand.

In chapter 9, I declare that God's words, as revealed in the Scriptures, are trustworthy. God's authoritative Word is inspired (inbreathed) by the Holy Spirit. This Word takes the "warp" out of our lives and sets us on the straight path. The Word of God is consistent and powerful, pulling down negative strongholds and making us complete in Him.

Chapter 10 deals with spiritual hunger. Hungry people must eat. The key word here is *hungry*. If you are not hungry, you won't consume any food. The Word of God is our spiritual food. It is appetizing and delightful to the taste of those who are hungry to know God. In this chapter, I offer you an overview, or a "bird's-eye view," of the Scriptures, connecting the dots between the Old Testament and the New, with the goal of creating that hunger in you. As I like to say, "Read the Bible till it reads you."

Chapter 11 deals with these questions: "How does the Bible 'work'? How does it connect you with heaven?" Without a doubt, the Bible is a unique Book. It is active and powerful. It changes and transforms you for God's purpose. It illuminates you, shining its truth into your inward parts, where evil is exposed and truth is revealed. It brings life and hope. It is the birthing place of faith and the starting point for healing. It cleanses and judges, and it is the mirror of revelation.

Chapter 12 concludes with a challenge: "Behold the Lord!" An argument without an experience is ineffective. Knowing God is not automatic; it is a lifelong process that requires dedication to the task. It is a lost art, and I have dedicated my life to bring it back to the people of God. Descriptions of this art—which includes prayer, meditation, and contemplation—are peppered throughout my writings. The secret place calls for you, and it is in that place where you encounter God. Too many people live "in the kitchen," like Martha, rather than "at the feet of Jesus," like Mary. In this chapter, as a bonus, I offer you keys to getting out of the kitchen and into a position of love in which you can receive God's Word at the feet of Jesus.

8

Knowing the Master Builder

Will your house stand or fall? What determines this?
In one word—foundation. Can you envision this?
The life with all the kinks and instabilities of self-will and
immaturity doesn't offer much in the way of groundwork upon
which to depend. But the ramrod, straightened lines of the life
brought into Kingdom relationship does.[18]
—Bob Mumford

Getting to know God is synonymous with building a life of faith, because God is the Master Builder. And if you want to know God's heart, then you must know His Word, where His nature and character are revealed. The Word speaks to you directly with His voice. I love the God of the Word—and I also love the Word of God!

I recall a story concerning the early childhood years of my late wife, Michal Ann Willard Goll. Her older Methodist Sunday school teacher, Mr. Tyler, taught her to love her Bible, to read it, to pray it, and to memorize it. She would sit on his lap, and he would tell her Bible stories, and this created a hunger for God within her heart. As she grew up, her Bible ended up becoming her "best friend."

---

18. Bob Mumford, *The King and You* (Old Tappan, NJ: Fleming H. Revell, 1974), 242.

One time, if I remember correctly, the Willard family was all loaded up in the station wagon ready to go on a trip somewhere. But Ann, the only daughter, was nowhere to be found. One of her brothers was sent back into the house to look for her. Well, there she was, nestled in her upstairs bedroom, quite contentedly doing her favorite thing—reading her Bible. What a way to grow up!

You see, you can have an actual relationship with the Word of God, the Bible, and this is a wonderful way to develop a relationship with God's Son Jesus, who is also known as the Word: *"In the beginning was the Word, and the Word was with God, and the Word was God....And the Word became flesh, and dwelt among us, and we saw His glory, glory as of the only begotten from the Father, full of grace and truth"* (John 1:1, 14; see also Revelation 19:13).

As we get to know the Bible, the Word of God, it will become the firm foundation upon which our faith is built. It will keep us from wandering away from God and going off in extreme directions. Derek Prince wrote about the importance of the Word for earnest believers who want to know God in a balanced way:

> In Genesis we read: "The Spirit of God was hovering over the face of the waters" (Gen. 1:2). In the next verse we read: "Then God said, 'Let there be light.'"
>
> That is, God's Word went forth; God pronounced the word *light*. And as the Word and the Spirit of God were thus united, creation took place, light came into being, and God's purpose was fulfilled.
>
> What was true of that great act of creation is true also of the life of each individual. God's Word and God's Spirit united in our lives contain all the creative authority and power of God Himself. Through them God will supply every need and will work out His perfect will and plan for us. But if we divorce these two from one another—seeking the Spirit without the Word, or studying the Word apart from the Spirit—we go astray and miss God's plan.[19]

---

19. Derek Prince, *The Spirit-Filled Believer's Handbook* (Lake Mary, FL: Creation House, 1993), 39.

If you want to know God well, you must have an actual relationship with His living Word, this Word that became flesh and dwelt among us, full of grace and truth. This will help you to trust in God more than you trust in what other people tell you. Other people will tell you that doctrine and denominations and church structures and exciting movements of God are the most important things. But what is most important is God Himself. (Now, please do not misunderstand me—I love the church. I have been a part of the church since childhood. Yet we have not been called to preach the gospel of the church but rather the gospel of the kingdom of God.)

Keeping Our Priorities Straight

Many, many times, people who have started with God have ended up going off on dead-end rabbit trails. They still think they know God, and they're proud of it, even somewhat defensive about it. But they have lost their living connection with Him (if they ever really had it in the first place). All they can talk about is how the church abused them, or the one or two insights that captured their attention at some point in time. They just can't fit the whole picture together. Maybe they lost perspective along the way because they removed themselves from the preaching of the Word. Guess what? Before I myself ever preach or teach, I still need to regularly read my Bible, and I always need to sit under others' anointed teaching of the Word of God to receive encouragement in my ongoing relationship with the living Word.

I am someone who highly values God's fresh, progressive revelation; I always want to seek more of it. But I have seen too many people who seem to think that the next great revelation will be some kind of improvement upon Jesus. Let me tell you, there is no revelation about God that is deeper than what you will find in the Word. Bottom line, there is no deeper truth than Jesus Christ crucified and risen from the dead. Let's keep to "the main and the plain"!

Christ is our foundation, our Rock. Whether you are part of a liturgical church or a nondenominational house church, the Scriptures and the ancient creeds of the church will keep you firmly rooted in God so that you will not "wobble." Any other foundation will eventually show itself as a form of humanism, because it will exalt a human personality, perhaps even an anointed human personality, above God Himself.

There is no revelation about God that is deeper than what you will find in the Word.

My earthly father was a carpenter who ran a lumberyard for most of his life, so you could say that I am the son of a carpenter, much like Jesus was. I grew up around the tools of the trade, which means I may have gleaned some insight from a natural perspective about knowing the Master Builder.

I have had many sad occasions to talk with people who have journeyed with God for a time, only to lose their "plumb line." A plumb line is a carpenter's tool that helps to keep a building straight and strong as it is being constructed. The prophet Amos had a vision in which God deployed His master plumb line to show that His people had fallen desperately short of His design. (See Amos 7:7–9.) I don't want that to happen to you. I don't want you to waste your life just because some flashy minister got you excited about his or her pet concept. I don't want you to give your devotion to something temporary.

In order to be unshakable, your faith must be built upon the covenant of God. Another way of saying this is that your life with God is built upon the books of God—the sixty-six remarkable books of the Bible that the Lord has given us to read, reread, and digest. This Word, composed of both the Old and the New Testaments (covenants), is *"living and active and sharper than any two-edged sword, and piercing as far as the division of soul and spirit, of both joints and marrow, and able to judge the thoughts and intentions of the heart"* (Hebrews 4:12).

Let's keep our priorities straight. The Father, Son, and Holy Spirit want you to become intimately familiar with the Word because, by doing so, you will get to know the One who inspired every line.

Christ Jesus, the Foundation Stone

As both the Old and New Testaments attest, the all-important, foundational Cornerstone is Jesus Christ Himself. If we do not build our faith on Him, we might as well be building it on sand. (See Matthew 7:24–27.) Jesus is the solid Rock.

In chapters 3 and 4 of this book, I gave you an overview of some of the three-hundred-plus prophetic Scriptures from the Old Testament that find their New Testament fulfillment in Jesus. Here are three more of these Scriptures, all of which have to do with Jesus the Rock, the Foundation Stone:

> So this is what the Sovereign LORD says: "See, I lay a stone in Zion, a tested stone, a precious cornerstone for a sure foundation; the one who relies on it will never be stricken with panic."   (Isaiah 28:16 NIV)

> The LORD is my rock, my fortress and my deliverer; my God is my rock, in whom I take refuge, my shield and the horn of my salvation, my stronghold.   (Psalm 18:2 NIV)

> My soul waits in silence for God only; from Him is my salvation. He only is my rock and my salvation, my stronghold; I shall not be greatly shaken.…My soul, wait in silence for God only, for my hope is from Him. He only is my rock and my salvation, my stronghold; I shall not be shaken. On God my salvation and my glory rest; the rock of my strength, my refuge is in God.   (Psalm 62:1–2, 5–7)

These passages foretell of Jesus' role as the firm-as-rock Foundation of the building of faith that believers spend their lives constructing. The Old Testament foretells—the New Testament reveals. Here is the Lord, the Rock, revealed in the New Testament:

> For no one can lay any foundation other than the one already laid, which is Jesus Christ.   (1 Corinthians 3:11 NIV)

> Jesus is "the stone you builders rejected, which has become the cornerstone." Salvation is found in no one else, for there is no other name

under heaven given to mankind by which we must be saved.

(Acts 4:11–12 NIV)

Now, therefore, you are no longer strangers and foreigners, but fellow citizens with the saints and members of the household of God, having been built on the foundation of the apostles and prophets, Jesus Christ Himself being the chief cornerstone, in whom the whole building, being fitted together, grows into a holy temple in the Lord.

(Ephesians 2:19–21 NKJV)

As you come to him, the living Stone—rejected by humans but chosen by God and precious to him—you also, like living stones, are being built into a spiritual house to be a holy priesthood, offering spiritual sacrifices acceptable to God through Jesus Christ. For in Scripture it says: "See, I lay a stone in Zion, a chosen and precious cornerstone, and the one who trusts in him will never be put to shame."

(1 Peter 2:4–6 NIV)

In three of the above passages, the New Testament writers were referring to the "cornerstone" prophecy from Isaiah, who did not know that a God-Man named Jesus would fulfill his words. The writers—Paul and Peter—added those details to the prophetic message. I especially love the adjectives that Peter applied to this Cornerstone: *"chosen"* and *"precious."* Other Bible translations use the words *"chief,"* *"elect,"* and *"honored."* (See NKJV, KJV, AMP.) That's our Jesus!

Christ Jesus, the Rock of Our Salvation

Jesus' own words confirm this truth that He is the Foundation Stone of our faith. Stay with me here as I explain what I mean. First, let's read Matthew's account of what Jesus said in this regard:

Now when Jesus came into the district of Caesarea Philippi, He was asking His disciples, "Who do people say that the Son of Man is?"… He said to them, "But who do you say that I am?" Simon Peter answered, "You are the Christ, the Son of the living God." And Jesus said to him, "Blessed are you, Simon Barjona, because flesh and blood did not reveal this to you, but My Father who is in heaven. I also say to you that you are Peter, and upon this rock I will build My church; and the gates of Hades will not overpower it."   (Matthew 16:13, 15–18)

Simon Peter captured the truth about Jesus, with the help of God's Spirit. It wasn't because Peter had studied it all out; it wasn't his good analysis or scholarship or research about history or the words of the prophets. It was a prophetic revelation. And Jesus praised Peter for expressing it so clearly, at the same time comparing him to a rock. However, Jesus did not call Peter the Rock, with a capital R. He was making a distinction between *petros*, Peter's name in Greek, which means "small stone," and *petra*, which means a massive rock, even a cliff.

We are not able to get this distinction from the English translation of both terms, which is the simple word *"rock."* Jesus was expressing, "I also say to you that you are *Petros* [small rock], and upon this *Petra* [i.e., Jesus the Christ, the Son of the living God] I will build My church." You could even say that Peter was "a chip off the old block"!

Jesus was doing a play on words here. He was happy to hear Peter's confession of the truth, but He was not confusing Peter with the Rock of Salvation (Himself). On the contrary, He was contrasting Peter with the Rock. The church would not be built, He said, upon a mere man (a pebble, by comparison), but rather on the One whom Peter had just confessed, the Rock (*Petra*) of Ages, which is immovable, unshakable, and utterly reliable. Peter was to be commended for recognizing and confessing the rock-solid truth about Jesus.

Peter's experience illustrates the way each individual believer starts to build on the foundation stone of the Rock of Salvation. It happens in four successive stages:

1. A direct, personal encounter with Jesus Christ. Jesus and Peter stood face-to-face. There was no middleman. No other human being played a part.

2. A direct, personal revelation about Jesus Christ—whether we understand where the information came from or not. Peter did not seem to realize that it was a divine revelation.

3. An acknowledgment of the truth of the revelation—a taking note of it.

4. A public confession of the truth. We cannot keep the truth a secret. We must confess it publicly, as Peter did, disregarding the possibility that we may have misunderstood. Only in so doing will we be able to receive Jesus' confirmation.

Replicating this pattern will ensure that we will avoid two possible outcomes, while guaranteeing a third. In regard to becoming a full disciple of Jesus, too many people settle for being what I call "careless sinners"—people who couldn't care less about salvation, who simply assume that their experience of life on earth is the whole story. Many others get partway—they come under conviction regarding their need for a Savior—but they do not enter into a true saving knowledge of Christ. Either of those two situations can be changed the moment a person has a direct, personal encounter with Jesus and responds as Peter did: "*You are the Christ, the Son of the living God*" (Matthew 16:16)!

---

*Jesus' own words confirm the truth that He is
the Foundation Stone of our faith.*

What Is Your Personal Experience?

Take a moment and think about your own experience. Have you encountered Jesus personally? (See John 16:13–14.) Have you met the One—the immovable, unchangeable Rock (see Hebrews 13:8)—upon whom your new life can be built? Has your eternal life begun? Referring to Himself in the third person in a prayer to the Father, Jesus affirmed, "*This is eternal life, that they may know You, the only true God, and Jesus Christ whom You have sent*" (John 17:3). Your eternal life does not begin when you go to heaven; it begins when you enter into a relationship with the living Son of God in the here and now. The more you get to know Him, the more experience of that eternal life you will have within you, until it reaches its fullness in eternity.

If you can confidently answer "Yes" to the questions in the previous paragraph, then you can say, along with John the Beloved Disciple, "*We know that the Son of God has come, and has given us understanding so that we may know Him who is true; and we are in Him who is true, in His Son Jesus Christ. This is the true God and eternal life*" (1 John 5:20). It's not merely a doctrine that you come to believe in—it's a *Person*. You know Him. And to know Him is to love Him.

You can entrust your very life into His hands. You can share Paul's sentiment when he wrote, "*I know whom I have believed and I am convinced that He is able to guard what I have entrusted to Him until that day*" (2 Timothy 1:12). But if you know only *what* you believe in, and not *whom*, the Foundation of your faith (the Cornerstone) has not yet been laid, and your faith will be easily shaken.

"*Now acquaint yourself with Him, and be at peace; thereby good will come to you*" (Job 22:21 NKJV). I like that translation of this verse. Acquaint yourself with God, and get to know Him, and you will never regret it.

Building a Solid Foundation

As I said at the beginning of this chapter, if you want to know God, you must know His Word, because as you get to know the Scriptures, they will become the firm foundation upon which your faith is built. Jesus, the Rock, is the all-important Cornerstone. Without Him, our faith cannot build us up into strong dwelling places for God.

Did you know that you are God's "building"? In the Bible, we find that believers are compared to houses, temples, and other constructions, all of which must begin with a firm foundation. Paul wrote the following words to the Christians in Corinth and Colossae:

> *For we are co-workers in God's service; you are God's field, God's building. By the grace God has given me, I laid a foundation as a wise builder, and someone else is building on it. But each one should build with care.*   (1 Corinthians 3:9–10 NIV)

> *As you have therefore received Christ Jesus the Lord, so walk in Him, rooted and built up in Him and established in the faith, as you have been taught.* (Colossians 2:6–7 NKJV)

While it is vital that each one of us build ourselves up in our faith (see Jude 20), individual believers cannot stand alone. We must combine our faith-energies so that, together, as the church, we become the dwelling place of God. Paul was explicit about this reality:

> *...built on the foundation of the apostles and prophets, with Christ Jesus himself as the chief cornerstone. In him the whole building is joined together and rises to become a holy temple in the Lord. And in him you too are being built together to become a dwelling in which God lives by his Spirit.* (Ephesians 2:20–22 NIV)

God will help us to construct this building like careful bricklayers, having laid down the *"elementary principles"* of Christ properly, so that the rest of the construction can proceed smoothly:

> *Therefore, leaving the discussion of the elementary principles of Christ, let us go on to perfection, not laying again the foundation of repentance from dead works and of faith toward God, of the doctrine of baptisms, of laying on of hands, of resurrection of the dead, and of eternal judgment. And this we will do if God permits.* (Hebrews 6:1–3 NKJV)

While we may not need to review the basics of the faith, such as repentance, forgiveness, and faithfulness, we need to build on them, striving for maturity and righteousness—which, of course, cannot be achieved in our own strength, but only through the generous grace of God. We pray for each other as Paul prayed for the elders of the church at Ephesus: *"So now, brethren, I commend you to God and to the word of His grace, which is able to build you up and give you an inheritance among all those who are sanctified"* (Acts 20:32 NKJV).[20]

---

20. To further explore the essential building blocks of the faith, see James Goll, *A Radical Faith* and *A Radical Faith Study Guide*.

Staying Strong

We need to listen to the Spirit of God and obey whatever He indicates that we should do (or not do). This is how we build and grow. The following is literally how the Word (Jesus Himself) explains it:

Therefore everyone who hears these words of Mine, and acts on them, may be compared to a wise man who built his house on the rock. And the rain fell, and the floods came, and the winds blew and slammed against that house; and yet it did not fall, for it had been founded on the rock. Everyone who hears these words of Mine and does not act on them, will be like a foolish man who built his house on the sand. The rain fell, and the floods came, and the winds blew and slammed against that house; and it fell—and great was its fall.   (Matthew 7:24–27)

Notice the difference between the ones called *"wise"* and the ones called *"foolish."* They all hear the same words, the words of Jesus, don't they? But not everyone follows through. Some people don't act on the direct words of the Word. Sadly, they may live to regret it, but by then it may be too late. Others are too quick to give up in the face of troubles, failing to understand that this lifelong building endeavor is not meant to be a walk in the park. Building your house is hard work, and you *will* suffer setbacks and unforeseen circumstances.

What do you do when you get knocked off your ladder, so to speak? You just get back up and try again. You ask God to show you how. You encourage other believers to continue in the faith, too. You keep reminding others that we can enter the kingdom of God only through this process of conquering difficulties. (See Acts 14:22.) Somehow, the repeated downs—and ups—constitute part of the building process itself, and your faith will get stronger because of your having faced all the trials.

Some would say I have been knocked around a bit by life's circumstances. I went through eight-plus years of battling non-Hodgkin's lymphoma cancer while, at the same time, my wife was being hit hard with colon cancer. Eventually, I won my war on this side—and Michal Ann won on the other side. Today, she is worshipping Jesus unabated before His very throne, and I know that we will be separated for only a short while.

When the winds and waves came slamming against my life, how did I survive the storms? Why am I not a hopeless casualty of shipwreck? Good question. The answer is that I learned how to drop the anchor of God's Word, while keeping it tethered to the ship of my life, even as I was being tossed around fiercely by uncertain circumstances.

Perhaps I have made it into the place called "safe harbor" because I did not lean on my own understanding. In all my ways, I acknowledged God, and He directed my path. (See Proverbs 3:5–6.) God's Word has become a lamp to my feet and a light to my path. (See Psalm 119:105.) From the very words of the Bible, I have learned to lean into the "wonderful words of life" (the theme of an old gospel song).[21] You, too, can be sustained and empowered by every word that proceeds from the mouth of God. (See Deuteronomy 8:3; Matthew 4:4.) Let His Word become your daily bread.

Proof of Discipleship

Keeping God's Word is the ultimate feature that distinguishes a true disciple from a non-disciple. Do you know the Word well enough to obey consistently? By that I mean, Do you know the written Word *and* do you know the Word Himself, Christ Jesus? Do you *love* the written Word and the Word Himself?

To know Him is to love Him, this One called the Word, who became flesh. If you want to deepen your relationship with God, develop a relationship with His Word. Listen, read, ingest, follow. Be responsive to His whispers. Talk with Him. Expect Him to communicate with you, because He will.

He will come and dwell with you, even as you continue to put the finishing touches on the well-built dwelling place you have been constructing for Him. This is what Jesus told His first disciples:

> *Just a little while now, and the world will not see Me any more, but you will see Me; because I live, you will live also. At that time [when that day comes] you will know [for yourselves] that I am in My Father, and you [are] in Me, and I [am] in you. The person who has My commands*

21. Philip P. Bliss, "Wonderful Words of Life," 1874.

and keeps them is the one who [really] loves Me; and whoever [really]
loves Me will be loved by My Father, and I [too] will love him and will
show (reveal, manifest) Myself to him. [I will let Myself be clearly seen
by him and make Myself real to him.] Judas, not Iscariot, asked Him,
Lord, how is it that You will reveal Yourself [make Yourself real] to us
and not to the world? Jesus answered, If a person [really] loves Me, he
will keep My word [obey My teaching]; and My Father will love him,
and We will come to him and make Our home (abode, special dwelling
place) with him.   (John 14:19–23 AMP)

When Jesus dwells with you, and you dwell with Him, this is called
"abiding in Him." Jesus' Beloved Disciple wrote to members of the early
church, "*Whoever keeps His word, truly the love of God is perfected in him. By*
this we know that we are in Him. He who says he abides in Him ought himself
also to walk just as He walked" (1 John 2:5–6 NKJV).

If you want to deepen your relationship with God, develop a relationship with His Word.

As we continue our exploration of discovery, we will keep on studying
God's Word and getting to know *Him*. (Again, the written Word is alive—
more like a person than just an "old book.") Our ever-developing relationship with God encompasses everything from one-on-one communication
with Him (our personal prayer life), to prophetic words received from the
Holy Spirit, to the confirming written Word. The Spirit and the Word
always agree—always have and always will. Since Creation (and from eternity), God's Word and God's Spirit have worked in unity and harmony.

What blueprint are you following in the construction of your spiritual
house? Are you after a quick fixer-upper? Or are you allowing the deepen-
ing work of the Holy Spirit, in union with the Word of God, to build a
house that can stand firm through any trial, test, or trauma this life may
throw at you?

Let's allow God to work in us and through us to establish and build a
perfect dwelling place! The resounding words of the old songs say it best:
"My hope is built on nothing less than Jesus' blood and righteousness;...

9

God's Trustworthy Word

Our faith is not dependent upon human knowledge and scientific
advance, but upon the unmistakable message of the Word of God.[24]
—Billy Graham

A re there any absolutes? Any standards or parts of the moral code that
do not change? Most of the world seems to think that we are becoming more enlightened as time goes on, and that this means we must
leave old standards behind. In the Western world, "inclusiveness" reigns
supreme. If you stand for absolutes, you are accused of being old-fashioned
and not progressive enough. Even some Christians accuse other believers
who hold to absolutes of having a "religious spirit" and of not understanding true love, mercy, and grace. Well, I guess, count me in!

Consider the erosion and shifting of values that has transpired in family television programming over the past generation or two. We went from
Father Knows Best, where honor governed in the home, to *Three's Company*,
which promoted a casual approach to virtue in male-female relationships,
to the very popular *Friends*, which depicted swapping partners and cheat-
ing as normal. Then we arrived at *The New Normal*, where same-sex partners are the new family unit. Huh? What happened?

24. Billy Graham, foreword to *What the Bible Is All About*, by Henrietta C. Mears (Ventura,
CA: Regal Books, 1999), 9.

In the political landscape of the United States, we have quickly moved away from the Defense of Marriage Act to embracing and sanctioning same-sex marriages. Part of the problem today is that a large part of the so-called Protestant church no longer believes that the Bible is the inspired Word of God because "higher criticism" knows better. The Ten Commandments are really the "Ten Suggestions." (You knew that, didn't you?) No wonder absolute truth is out the window.

I, for one, am here to say that absolutes have not changed in God's inspired, authoritative Word, the Bible. You can trust the God of the Word, and you can trust the Word of God.

The Bible—So Much More

I like to talk about the Bible as much as I like to talk about the One who put it together. It's so much more than a storybook, even though it's true that it contains one story after another. As I have been pointing out, Jesus, the Son of God, is also known as the Word (remember John 1:1), which connects Him closely to the Bible, the Word of God.

Let's take a fresh look at God's Word, starting out with the words of Jesus the Word, as recorded in the Word!

The Authoritative Word

The disciple John wrote down Jesus' reply to a group of Jewish men who were unhappy with Him because He had called Himself the Son of God, which they considered blasphemy.

> *Has it not been written in your Law, "I said, you are gods"? If he called them gods, to whom the word of God came (and the Scripture cannot be broken), do you say of Him, whom the Father sanctified and sent into the world, 'You are blaspheming,' because I said, "I am the Son of God"?*
> (John 10:34–36)

I want you to notice how Jesus referred to the Word here. First, He called it *"your Law."* By that, He meant the Scriptures as the Jews knew them—the books that we call the Old Testament.[25] (He was quoting from Psalm 82:6, which they probably knew by heart. That verse goes on to say, *"And all of you are sons of the Most High."*) The *"Law,"* in other words, did not refer only to the first five books of our Bible, known to Jews as the Torah, but also to all the rest of the books that had been collected as Scripture to date, including the Psalms. "The Law" was a broad term for the whole collection, referring to a wider range of books than just the ones that laid down rules and regulations.

Then Jesus said of the psalmist and the psalmist's original audience, *"If...[these] to whom the word of God came...."* Thus, we can see that Jesus recognized that the Psalms and the rest of the known Scriptures were the very *"word of God."* This simple term reveals a lot. It shows that the truths expressed in Scripture do not have their origin with men but rather are God-inspired. Although God has used many human instruments to compose the Bible, there is really one main source. That's why it's called the Word of God—not the word of John, the word of Peter, the word of Isaiah, and so forth. It's the Word of God Himself.

So, within two related sentences, Jesus referred to the *"Law," "the word of God,"* and *"the Scripture,"* all three being equivalent. The word *"Scripture"* means "that which is written." From this, we learn that the Bible does not contain the entire knowledge of God but rather is the authoritative portion of the vast spoken words of God for humankind that has been recorded in writing.

I find it very interesting to see that Jesus added *"and the Scripture cannot be broken."* That brief statement contains within it every claim for supreme and divine authority that can ever be made on behalf of the Bible. It doesn't mean only that the truths are unbreakable and unchanging. It means, for instance, that if you break one of the Ten Commandments, you have not done any damage at all to the Word of God. The Scripture is so unbreakable that it breaks *you* if you try to break its truths. You cannot shift the Word of God. Its authority is absolute. You can't beat it. Disobedience to it brings consequences. Don't forget that!

---

25. Many other biblical passages make it clear that "the Law" is equivalent to "Scripture," such as John 8:17; 12:34; 15:25; Romans 3:19; 1 Corinthians 14:21.

The truths expressed in Scripture do not have their origin with men but rather are God-inspired.

Inspired by the Holy Spirit

The entire Word of God has been inspired directly by the Spirit of God, as we read in Paul's letter to Timothy (he was referring solely to our Old Testament, since the New Testament was just beginning to be written then): *"All scripture is given by inspiration of God, and is profitable for doctrine, for reproof, for correction, for instruction in righteousness"* (2 Timothy 3:16 KJV). The word translated *"inspiration of God"* is the Greek word *theopneustos*, which means "divinely breathed in," "God-breathed," or "inspired by God." *Theopneustos* is derived from two other Greek words: *theos*, meaning "God," and *pneo*, meaning "to blow," or "to breathe hard." The word *pneo* is also connected to the Greek word for "spirit," *pneuma*, which literally means "wind" or "breath." The Holy Spirit is the invisible and unerring influence who controlled and directed the men who wrote down the different books that we collectively call the Bible.

Again, this Spirit-inspired Book will take the warp out of our lives. It will set our course straight and keep us from deviating from the path of righteousness. Light comes into your soul when you read the words of the Bible. If you put it away and stop looking at it, darkness can reenter your soul; but the more you keep this Book in front of you, the more training in righteousness you receive.

How many of us have said something like the following: "Lord, I would love to have a mentor to help me"? Well, let me commend Isaiah to you as a mentor. And Moses. And Elijah. And an old woman named Anna, whom you can read about in the gospel of Luke. And various members of the early church, whose lives model godliness through the pages of the Acts of the Apostles and the epistles to the various churches.

When I think about the mentors in my own life, most of them have not been physically present with me. My primary mentors have been the authors of books, and that includes the books of the Bible. I can make that statement honestly, even though my life has been filled with the presence of so many anointed men and women of God. None of them has mentored me better than the people in the Bible, collectively—which means that the Word Himself is my best Mentor. In fact, the Bible is my friend. Let me tell you a story in this regard.

Years ago, when I was on staff at a major church in Kansas City, Missouri, I completed a counseling session in a second-floor office. (I used to move around from place to place instead of having just one primary office.) When I vacated the room, I unknowingly left my brown leather *New American Standard Bible* in that room. I loved that Bible. I read it day and night. It was all marked up, and no other Bible read like "my" Bible. It was my constant companion.

Afterward, when I could not locate my Bible, I felt lost. I tried reading other Bibles, but they just did not feel the same. Apparently having no other option, I attempted to move on and adapt to another version. Weeks later, I happened to go back into that upstairs office. There it was—my Bible. It was lying right where I had left it. I remember picking up that worn Bible with the Moody imprint on its spine, walking out into the hallway, and praising the Lord out loud. Kissing my Bible, and filled with glee, I exclaimed, "I found my friend! I found my friend! I found my friend!"

You see, my Bible was and is much more than a book to me. It was and is my friend and companion in life.

Moved by the Holy Spirit

Not only has the Holy Spirit inspired the written Word, but He also inspires fresh words to this day. Such words never carry the same level of authority as the written Word, but that does not invalidate them. It's just that, as Peter and John wrote, the Spirit must verify any word from God and help us to understand it.

> But know this first of all, that no prophecy of Scripture is a matter of one's own interpretation, for no prophecy was ever made by an act of human will, but men moved by the Holy Spirit spoke from God.
>
> (2 Peter 1:20–21)

Beloved, do not believe every spirit, but test the spirits to see whether they are from God, because many false prophets have gone out into the world. (1 John 4:1)

On our own, we can't interpret even our own Spirit-inspirations. We need confirmation and direction from the written Word, which we can trust is thoroughly God-directed. The Greek word in the passage from 2 Peter that is translated *"moved by"* can also be rendered "directed their course by [had their course directed by]" or "borne along by." It's like sailing: Without the wind (we could say Wind), the sailboat doesn't go anywhere.

God controlled the human "vessels" who wrote the Scriptures by the interplay of His divine Spirit with their spiritual, emotional, mental, and physical faculties. When the Spirit breathed on them, they were blown out of the natural realm into the supernatural. They sailed over into revelation.

The Purified Word

By the time the Psalms were written, people had long been creating valuable objects out of silver. When the silver came out of the ground, it was impure, mixed with other elements. After being mined, each lump of stuff would be purified in a clay furnace or oven. David had that in mind when he wrote this line about God's words:

The words of the LORD are pure words, like silver tried in a furnace of earth, purified seven times. (Psalm 12:6 NKJV)

The furnace made of earth (clay) represents the human element, while the silver represents the divine message. The fire ensures the absolute purity of the silver—that is, the message—and the notation *"seven times"* indicates the complete and perfect work of the Holy Spirit. (Seven is considered the number of completion or perfection.) As you will remember from the tongues of fire on the day of Pentecost, the Holy Spirit can be represented as a burning fire, as well as a wind. Spirit-fire-purified words are perfectly pure. Therefore, the Holy Spirit, while burning inside human hearts, overruled human frailties and errors in producing the divine message of Scripture.

The Consistency of Scripture

It's been settled—the Word of the Lord, that is: *"Forever, O LORD, Your word is settled in heaven"* (Psalm 119:89). When the psalmist wrote that line, he wanted to emphasize that the Word of God is not a product of time but of eternity. Eternity goes both ways—clear back to Genesis 1 (and beyond), and forward to the heavenly drama of John's Revelation (and beyond).

This was the testimony of Jesus, as well. He said, *"Heaven and earth will pass away, but My words will not pass away"* (Matthew 24:35). Even if all the elements of heaven or earth pass away, His words will hold firm; they cannot be destroyed. They stand through all the tests of time and eternity. No cataclysmic event or ignorant interpretation can obliterate God's words. Forever, they remain as the standard of life.

Such was Jesus' confidence in the effectiveness and strength of the written Word that He selected certain Scriptures to cut down the lying temptations of Satan. During His forty-day wilderness sojourn, He confronted the devil's temptations with direct quotes from Scripture. Each time, He said, *"It is written…"* and proceeded to quote a line from the book of Deuteronomy. (See Matthew 4:1–11; Luke 4:1–13.)

Even Satan did not deny the absolute authority of Scripture. This shows us that the darkest evil is under subjection to the Word of God, which should be good news to those who adhere to the Scriptures. Is it because there is magic in those particular words? Not at all. It's because there is a God in heaven who sits on the throne of the universe, and He is the Author of the words in this Book. His invincible authority stands behind the Word of God. The Bible is not just a collection of good teachings, although it is that. It has *power* when written or spoken.

God's invincible authority stands behind His Word.
Even the darkest evil is under subjection to it.

You see, Jesus did not differentiate between the authority of the scriptural books according to their age or their attribution to a particular human author. Nor did He set aside the ancient words in favor of new writings. In His Sermon on the Mount, He made His case:

> *Do not think that I came to destroy the Law or the Prophets. I did not come to destroy but to fulfill. For assuredly, I say to you, till heaven and earth pass away, one jot or one tittle will by no means pass from the law till all is fulfilled.* (Matthew 5:17–18 NKJV)

Jesus was saying that the original text of Hebrew Scripture is so accurate and so authoritative that not even one jiggle of the scribe's pen can change it. Not the smallest letter or stroke will pass from the law until all of it is accomplished, because Jesus has come as Messiah to fulfill it. In the Hebrew alphabet, a *"jot"* is the smallest letter of all. It looks like an inverted comma. And a *"tittle"* indicates a little curl that is even smaller than the jot. Even the jots and tittles will stand firm—they cannot be erased or altered—until God's complete plan has been played out. The Scripture and its Author together are our absolute source of life. Whenever people or cultures veer away from God, they are at risk of collapse; they are standing on shifting sand.

Over and over, Jesus used the strength of the authority of the Word against His enemies, and they could not refute Him. Once, He was being grilled by some Sadducees about points of the Law. They thought they had Him on the matter of the resurrection of the dead, which they adamantly refused to believe in. (They always remind me of the people today who relegate the realm of the supernatural to the rank of fairy tales.) They were good Jews of their day, and they were religious leaders. They knew their Torah. So Jesus quoted from something they knew, the book of Exodus, picking up in the midst of the account of Moses and the burning bush, which reads, "I am the God of your father, the God of Abraham, the God of Isaac, and the God of Jacob" (Exodus 3:6). Here's how Jesus used the quote:

> *Regarding the resurrection of the dead, have you not read what was spoken to you by God: "I am the God of Abraham, and the God of Isaac, and the God of Jacob"? He is not the God of the dead but of the living.* (Matthew 22:31–32)

By using the phrase *"spoken to you by God,"* Jesus once again confirmed and authenticated the Old Testament as the Word of God. He quoted a passage that was fifteen centuries old but that had not lost any of its vitality, accuracy, authority, or efficacy. He quoted it without changing a jot or a tittle.

In regard to challenges from the Sadducees' rival group, the Pharisees, Jesus once responded to their quizzing Him about divorce. What did God think of it? What was the truth? Once again, Jesus referred to Scriptures that they knew well. He began, *"Have you not read…?"* referring to the book of Genesis obliquely:

> *Have you not read that He who created them from the beginning made them male and female, and said, "For this reason a man shall leave his father and mother and be joined to his wife, and the two shall become one flesh"? So they are no longer two, but one flesh. What therefore God has joined together, let no man separate.*
>
> (Matthew 19:4–6)

"In Beginning" was the Hebrew title of the book of Genesis, so Jesus' questioners knew what He was talking about. And by saying, *"He who created them from the beginning…said,…"* Jesus was once again verifying that every detail of the Scriptures should be considered God's Word. He remained completely consistent in His use of the written Word as the final authority on every matter, whether He was resisting temptation, facing persecution, or refuting opponents in a debate.

"That the Scripture May Be Fulfilled"

In the previous chapter of this book, and also in chapters 4 and 5, I gave you examples of Old Testament prophetic words that were clearly fulfilled by Jesus' life, ministry, death, burial, and resurrection. I find it remarkable the way these ancient words can be paired so perfectly with later events, thus demonstrating the validity of the Word. Even when we have not yet seen a particular fulfillment with our own eyes, we can trust that the words foretelling it are true.

This was a definitive point of reference for Jesus. Consider, for example, the town He chose as His home base. Matthew 4:12–17 tells about the beginnings of His ministry, when He withdrew into Galilee, leaving Nazareth behind and settling in the region of Capernaum. Matthew mentions that this was the fulfillment of Isaiah 9:1–2, which designated that particular location as one to which the Messiah would come, as well as described Christ's mission to shine as a light in the darkness.

Jesus knew all the Scriptures that pointed to Him as the Messiah, and, as we noted previously, after His resurrection, He cited them on the road to Emmaus to two of His downcast disciples, who hadn't yet recognized who He was. *"Then beginning with Moses and with all the prophets, He explained to them the things concerning Himself in all the Scriptures"* (Luke 24:27).

The prophets whose words are recorded in the Old Testament specifically and accurately predicted each of the following incidents in the earthly life of Jesus the Messiah: His birth to a virgin mother at Bethlehem, His flight into Egypt, His home in Nazareth, His anointing by the Holy Spirit, His ministry in Galilee, His healing of the sick, the rejection by the Jews of His teaching and miracles, His use of parables, His being betrayed by a friend, His being forsaken by His disciples, His being hated without a cause, His being condemned along with criminals, His garments' being parceled out by lot to others, His being offered vinegar to quench His thirst on the cross, His body's being pierced without His bones being broken, His burial in a rich man's tomb, and His resurrection from the dead on the third day. Most of these prophetic fulfillments will sound familiar to you, especially since we reviewed so many of them in chapters 4 and 5 of this book. Again and again, the Word proves true.

You Can Trust the God of the Word

The earthly life of Jesus was guided in every aspect by the authority and prophetic influence of God's Word. The Word of God is cohesive, complete, and all-sufficient. From Genesis to Revelation, it unfolds the nature and consequences of sin, along with the way of deliverance from sin and its consequences—through faith in the Lord Jesus Christ. As we heed these words and obey them, we will find and receive true, abundant, and eternal life.

Let the consistency and reliability of the Scriptures encourage you as you think about knowing God better, because He obviously *makes Himself known* in countless ways, and the Bible is one of His primary means. He is not hiding or keeping Himself remote and secret.

Instead of neglecting the written Word out of apathy or ignorance of its value, we need to devour it, if we want to know its Author. Let the Word of God be your companion and friend. Believe me, there will always be something new to discover in it—for the rest of your life!

Great news, indeed. You have a lifetime to spend getting to know God by getting to know His Word.

10

Hungry for His Every Word

As the bread of life we eat it, we feed on it. In eating our daily
bread the body takes in the nourishment, which visible nature, the
sun and the earth, prepared for us in the seed corn. We assimilate
it, and it becomes our very own, part of ourselves; it is our life.
In feeding on the Word of God the powers of the Heavenly life
enter into us, and become our very own; we assimilate them, they
become a part of ourselves, the life of our life.[26]
—Andrew Murray

At the end of the previous chapter, I declared that we must *devour* the
Word of God if we want to know God better. I don't think I stated it
too strongly. Ask yourself, "Am I *that* hungry for the Word?" If you're not
famished for more, ask God to give you a greater desire for it. If you're not
hungry enough, you won't eat enough. Again, hungry people must eat. And
just as eating nourishing food on a daily basis makes you physically strong
and healthy, so absorbing the Word daily renews you spiritually.

You could start by reading something as an "appetizer." Read this
chapter to help increase your hunger for the Word of God. You want to
be able to tune your ear to God and lean into Him, cherishing His Word

26. Andrew Murray, *The Best of Andrew Murray* (Grand Rapids, MI: Baker Book House,
1994), 46.

in your heart. Your spiritual hunger will make reading and studying His Word, praying, and seeking Him a delight. Sheer dutifulness will not provide or sustain the same degree of motivation. Christians who have an "I ought to" attitude will never get much out of God's Word. However, if you are ravenous for the Word, you will automatically become more relational. When you want more of something, you're willing to expend some energy to get it. You will reach out to the Word and to God Himself to satisfy your need, and you will be grateful to Him when you receive something. Into the bargain, you will get to know God a little better each time you consume another morsel of the well-balanced scriptural meal that He offers you.

Finding Jesus in Every Book of the Bible

Perhaps you have suppressed or redirected your spiritual hunger. Maybe you didn't understand that your yearning for satisfaction could be met in God, so you have spent most of your life trying to find happiness in human relationships, entertainment, and/or a career. Possibly, the very last place you would expect to find gratification for your inner ache would be a thick book with a black cover that seemingly doesn't make much sense to you.

Of course, you have probably heard various objections to reading the Bible; you may have expressed some of them yourself, such as the following: "It's too hard to understand." "Who cares about all those 'begat's' and 'begot's'?" "Why read the book of Leviticus if all those rules don't apply anymore?" "The whole book is just, like, 'Huh?'" "It gets really boring in places." "That book of Job—what an epic bummer." "I really don't see what all the fuss is about. I just never can get anything out of the Bible—sorry."

I, too, once thought I'd never get anything out of some books of the Bible. But I'm here to tell you that I have found Jesus in every one, even those that seemed the least likely. Believe me, anyone who wants to know God better will find Him most directly and easily in the pages of this Book. In fact, any attempt to understand God and His ways *without* the

Word of God is fruitless. The Bible is God's revelation of Himself to humankind.

The Bible is your guidebook. It tells you, "This is the way to walk and to talk and to pray. This is how you 'do' life. Read this, and you will live a long and overcoming life." It is like an extended love letter from your Father in heaven. It really is.

If you don't believe me, I guess you'd better start reading it in order to prove me wrong!

Anyone who wants to know God better will find Him most directly and easily in the pages of the Bible.

Take a Minute

Let's take a minute to review what we just discussed in the previous chapter: The Bible is a record of God's words to human beings, written down by men who were *"moved by the Holy Spirit"* (2 Peter 1:21). Since it is the Word of God and not the word of humans, its power and authority originate with God Himself. Its words carry all the integrity and dependability of God. *"All Scripture is inspired by God"* (2 Timothy 3:16); it is *"God-breathed"* (2 Timothy 3:16 NIV, AMP).

What does this Book consist of? The following is a quick overview of "The Greatest Book Ever Written." It is a collection of sixty-six books that were written down by approximately forty-four inspired authors over a period spanning 1,600 years. The books have been divided into two parts—the Old Testament and the New Testament. The Old Testament comprises thirty-nine books; their content spans the time period from the Creation of the world to the return of the Israelites from the Babylonian exile. The New Testament contains twenty-seven books; these cover the time from Jesus' birth to the end of the first century (with the last book, Revelation, foretelling our present day and the time to come).

The Old Testament

The thirty-nine books of the Old Testament can be divided into five major categories: (1) the Law, or the Pentateuch (the five books written by Moses); (2) history; (3) poetry and wisdom; (4) the Major Prophets; and (5) the Minor Prophets. These books contain the story of God's dealings with His chosen people, the Israelites, and they are recognized by Jews to this day as their Scriptures, God's sacred Word to the Jewish people.

Here is a list of the names of the books that fall into each of the five categories:

THE LAW (PENTATEUCH)

Genesis	Numbers
Exodus	Deuteronomy
Leviticus	

HISTORY

Joshua	1 and 2 Chronicles
Judges	Ezra
Ruth	Nehemiah
1 and 2 Samuel	Esther
1 and 2 Kings	

POETRY AND WISDOM

Job	Ecclesiastes
Psalms	Song of Solomon
Proverbs	

MAJOR PROPHETS

Isaiah	Ezekiel
Jeremiah	Daniel
Lamentations	

MINOR PROPHETS

Hosea	Nahum
Joel	Habakkuk
Amos	Zephaniah
Obadiah	Haggai
Jonah	Zechariah
Micah	Malachi

Most of the Old Testament was originally written in Hebrew (a Semitic language akin to Arabic). Small segments of Ezra and Daniel and one verse in Jeremiah were written in Aramaic, another Semitic tongue that was the language of Palestine in Jesus' day.

Remarkably, verification of the historical details recorded in the Old Testament keeps turning up in the archaeological record. One significant example concerns the Hittites, a group of people who were named forty-seven times in the Old Testament but were not mentioned by that name in any other ancient inscriptions. In the late nineteenth century, skeptical scholars used to point to this "mythical" kingdom as proof that one could not trust the Bible as a record of history. Then, in 1906, a German archaeologist unearthed the ruins of a large city in modern-day Turkey that proved to have been the capital of the vast Hittite empire. The Old Testament record had been vindicated.[27] The discovery of this kind of archaeological proof has occurred over and over.

It's helpful to know a bit about the history of how the Bible was composed. Although, at first, the revelations of God were passed down by oral tradition, God later commanded that what He had spoken should be written down: *"Then the LORD said to Moses, 'Write down these words, for in accordance with these words I have made a covenant with you and with Israel'"* (Exodus 34:27). Subsequently, significant events and people in the history of Israel were marked by a written record, along with what God did or spoke through the prophets. (See, for example, Numbers 33:2; Deuteronomy 17:18; Joshua 24:26; 1 Samuel 10:25; Isaiah 8:16; Jeremiah 36:2.) These writings became the Holy Scriptures to the people of God,

---

27. Merrill F. Unger, *Unger's Bible Dictionary* (Chicago: Moody Press, 1966), 576–577.

and God expected them to revere them as such. (See, for example, Joshua 1:8; Psalm 1:2.) They have been passed down to this day and remain sacred to both Jews and Christians.

When you read any part of the Old Testament, it is important to realize that all the books in it (even the ancient history) look *forward*. When Adam and Eve sinned, God promised a Redeemer. (See Genesis 3:15.) The prophets kept painting details of the life of the expected future Messiah. Although some of the books scarcely allude to Jesus, nevertheless, you can find Him in every one of the thirty-nine books of the Old Testament, if you know what to look for. In other words, the Old Testament can generally be summarized as the history of the nation of Israel, always declaring God's promise that He would send a Redeemer to purchase the salvation of people who were "walking in darkness."

Among other things, this certainly shows us the Father's heart. He has been longing from the earliest days for a people He could call His own, and He has been amazingly generous to give Himself for the sake of ever-sinful human beings.

All the books in the Old Testament look forward—
to the coming Messiah.

The New Testament

Eight or nine authors wrote the twenty-seven books of the New Testament over a period of about fifty years. The New Testament can be divided into five types of books: (1) the Gospels; (2) early church history; (3) the epistles (letters) of Paul; (4) the general epistles (letters written by others); and (5) prophecy. The Gospels—Matthew, Mark, Luke, and John—record the circumstances of Jesus' earthly life, along with a lot of His teachings. Luke's second book, the Acts of the Apostles, narrates a history of the early church. The epistles are letters from some of the apostles to various churches and individuals, mainly explaining Christian doctrines. Revelation is John's record of a vision of the end times that he received while he was in exile on the Isle of Patmos.

Here is how the books line up:

THE GOSPELS

Matthew   Luke

Mark   John

EARLY CHURCH HISTORY

Acts

THE EPISTLES OF PAUL

Romans   Colossians

1 and 2 Corinthians   1 and 2 Thessalonians

Galatians   1 and 2 Timothy

Ephesians   Titus

Philippians   Philemon

THE GENERAL EPISTLES

Hebrews   1, 2, and 3 John

James   Jude

1 and 2 Peter

PROPHECY

Revelation

All these books were written in Greek, which was the *lingua franca* (common language) of the Eastern Mediterranean countries. The apostles and others used Koine Greek, from which today's Greek language arose. Koine Greek is no longer used today except in the study of ancient manuscripts. Therefore, its word meanings and usages have been essentially frozen in time, which can be viewed as an advantage when disputes arise over the precise meanings of scriptural terminology (because the word meanings cannot have changed over time through continued use).

Greek was the predominant language of the Roman Empire, although the people of Palestine, including Jesus, spoke Hebrew and Aramaic among themselves. The region was multicultural, and the people were multilingual. Educated people became fluent in speaking and understanding Greek, and many could read it and write it. This common language proved to be an invaluable tool in the speedy, early spread of the gospel message by both written and oral means.

We should remember that the first New Testament "Scripture" that anyone received in those days would have been oral, as believers preached the gospel message and recounted the developing story of the work of the Holy Spirit. Only later did the various written renderings start to be considered as authoritative as the rest of Scripture. Jesus and the early church would have applied the term "Scripture" only to the books of our Old Testament. Yet, when Paul commended those who received his teachings as the divinely inspired word of God and *"not as the word of men"* (1 Thessalonians 2:13), he was almost certainly referring to his verbal teachings. Moreover, in his second letter, Peter referred to Paul's epistles as Scripture: "[Paul's] *letters contain some things that are hard to understand, which ignorant and unstable people distort,* **as they do the other Scriptures,** *to their own destruction"* (2 Peter 3:16 NIV).

The first parts of the New Testament to be written down were epistles, especially those composed by Paul during his travels. Most of the letters to various churches and individuals were written from about the mid-40s to about the mid-60s. The Gospels were composed between about AD 60 and about AD 100, recorded from the inspired memories of those who had walked with Jesus when He was on the earth (or, as in the case of Luke, someone who had walked with Paul). These memories had been kept fresh by much verbal transmission; and, in a culture that relied on verbal communication more than on written communication, people's retention of verbal information was much better than ours is today—just another reason we can count on the accuracy of these vital words. It is generally believed that the entire New Testament had been inked onto papyrus or parchment by the end of the first century after Christ.

Yes…of course, the letters and books of the New Testament were penned by hand. This was long before the printing press was invented. Even paper as we know it today did not exist. Every copy of a manuscript had to be reproduced by hand. And they were replicated freely; it was a common practice among the first-century churches to share and exchange letters that the apostles had written. In fact, this practice was encouraged by Paul himself in his letter to the believers in the church in Colossae, to whom he wrote, "*After this letter has been read to you, see that it is also read in the church of the Laodiceans and that you in turn read the letter from Laodicea*" (Colossians 4:16 NIV).

Gradually, each local church began to accumulate copies of the various writings of the apostles. In order to "read" them, people had to come together to hear them read aloud. This is why Paul exhorted Timothy to attend to the public reading of the Scriptures, which, of course, would have included the ancient Scriptures as well as the newer manuscripts: "*Until I come, give attention to the public reading of Scripture, to exhortation and teaching*" (1 Timothy 4:13).

For centuries, nobody owned a personal Bible, let alone a personal pocket Bible. (They didn't have pockets yet, either, but that's another topic!) Obviously, there were no smartphones with apps that put the Scriptures, in multiple translations, at their fingertips. Even after Gutenberg's invention of the printing press in the fifteenth century, Bibles were so valuable and rare that most communities owned only one—and it was often chained to a stand in the church for safekeeping.

Just stop and think about that for a minute, in light of the avalanche of Bibles available to us in our own day. How many Bibles do you have in your home? Do you even know? I have never counted how many I have on my bookshelves alone; and these do not include the digital and online versions that I have access to. We are pretty casual about this treasure trove, aren't we? Now we can read the Word in our own language anytime we want to, instead of having to trudge over to the local church building to await a public reading. Celebrate your Word-wealth—take a Bible-reading break right now!

Progressive Revelation

I would be remiss if I did not add a word about the importance of interpreting the Old Testament in the light of the New. The Old Testament often cannot be understood without knowledge of the New Testament revelation of Christ. In other words, the Bible is a progressive revelation about God.

We have established the fact that the Old Testament is loaded with prophetic indications that foretell the coming of a Messiah at a future time. When we get to the New Testament, the Gospels detail the actual coming of the Messiah, and the epistles tell about what He accomplished through His death and resurrection, while also laying down a way of life based on the ongoing presence of His Spirit. The prophetic men who wrote the Old Testament under the inspiration of the Holy Spirit could not fully understand what they had written, because the Christ had not yet been revealed. (See 1 Peter 1:10–12.) Nobody reading the declarations of the Old Testament could have unraveled their complete meaning without knowing about Christ Jesus.

The Old Testament often cannot be understood without knowledge of the New Testament revelation of Christ.

Do you recall the story about the Ethiopian eunuch? (See Acts 8:26–40.) It perfectly illustrates my point. The Ethiopian, who was a devout Jew, was trying to understand the meaning of Isaiah 53, by which he was completely mystified. He needed the help of someone with a working knowledge of who the Messiah was. God came through for him.

Dispatched by an angel of God, the disciple named Philip ran to catch up with the fast-moving chariot of the eunuch, who was reading aloud from Isaiah at that very moment.

Philip ran up...and said, "Do you understand what you are reading?" And he said, "Well, how could I, unless someone guides me?" And he invited Philip to come up and sit with him. Now the passage of Scripture which he was reading was this: "He was led as a sheep to slaughter; and as a lamb before its shearer is silent, so He does not open His mouth. In humiliation His judgment was taken away; who will relate His generation? For His life is removed from the earth." The eunuch answered Philip and said, "Please tell me, of whom does the prophet say this? Of himself or of someone else?" Then Philip opened his mouth, and beginning from this Scripture he preached Jesus to him.

(Acts 8:30–35)

Philip used Isaiah's prophecy as a jumping-off point for telling the man about Jesus, the Lamb of God who had died for his sake. The heart of the Ethiopian eunuch was burning. God's love became alive to him—all because someone had interpreted the old words in the light of the new. This stranger who had joined him *knew* this Man whom Isaiah was writing about! The Ethiopian's response was immediate:

> *As they went along the road they came to some water; and the eunuch said, "Look! Water! What prevents me from being baptized?" [And Philip said, "If you believe with all your heart, you may." And he answered and said, "I believe that Jesus Christ is the Son of God."] And he ordered the chariot to stop; and they both went down into the water, Philip as well as the eunuch, and he baptized him.* (Acts 8:36–38)

Isn't that exciting? Progressive revelation is so rich! The knowledge of God increases substantially when you add the Jesus of the New Testament to the veiled words and visions of the Old Testament.

The Goal: "Read Your Bible Till It Reads You"!

"Read your Bible till it reads you"—that's an original James Goll-ism. I don't mean it as merely a catchy saying. It's true, because the more you pore over His Word, the more God bathes and permeates your mind and heart.

Paul wrote to his protégé Timothy (and therefore to us, as well), *"Study to show thyself approved unto God, a workman that needeth not to be ashamed, rightly dividing the word of truth"* (2 Timothy 2:15 KJV). We should be studying the Word diligently.

Every single believer needs to develop a thorough knowledge of the Word of God. As I have been stressing, to know the Word is to know its Author. His Word forms you into His image and sets you up in the abundant life. It washes the grime of the world off your soul and beams the light of heaven through you. If you read your Bible till it reads you, God's light will shine brighter and brighter in you as you mature in your faith. Your joy will grow. After a while, you won't simply be reading the epistles—you will have *become* an epistle of Christ to the people around you!

Here are at least eight distinct reasons why we should be diligent about studying the Word of God:

1. Jesus urged us to. For example, He said,

> *If you abide in Me, and My words abide in you, ask whatever you wish, and it will be done for you. My Father is glorified by this, that you bear much fruit, and so prove to be My disciples....If you keep My commandments, you will abide in My love; just as I have kept My Father's commandments and abide in His love.* (John 15:7–8, 10)

2. The Scriptures testify of Jesus. Jesus explained that while the Scriptures reveal who He is, we must search them with an open heart so that we can hear God's voice and allow His Word to dwell in us. Otherwise, we may not receive the truth that the Scriptures convey. (See John 5:37–40 NKJV.) Luke commended the actions of the Jews in Berea who *"were of more noble character than those in Thessalonica, for they received the message with great eagerness and examined the Scriptures every day to see if what Paul said was true. As a result, many of them believed"* (Acts 17:11–12 NIV).

3. It will enable us to spiritually flourish. Psalm 1:2–3 says, *"His delight is in the law of the LORD, and in His law he meditates day and night. He will be like a tree firmly planted by streams of water, which yields its fruit in its season and its leaf does not wither; and in whatever he does, he prospers."*

4. King Solomon, who was the wisest man of his day, emphasized the importance of knowing and heeding God's Word.

> *My son, pay attention to what I say; turn your ear to my words. Do not let them out of your sight, keep them within your heart; for they are life to those who find them and health to one's whole body.*
> (Proverbs 4:20–22 NIV)

5. King David (Solomon's father), who was "a man after God's own heart" (see 1 Samuel 13:14; Acts 13:22), set an example for pursuing God and His Word. For instance, He wrote, *"How precious to me are your* *thoughts, O God! How vast is the sum of them! Were I to count them, they would outnumber the grains of sand"* (Psalm 139:17–18 NIV).

6. It will enable us to establish a foundation for our faith. The apostle Peter urged believers to desire the *"milk"* of the Word (see 1 Peter 2:2), which involves learning the facts portrayed in the Scriptures and understanding how these things relate to one another. While we are in the "milk" stage, we should begin to be able to identify the main themes that run through the pages of the Bible, the matters of faith that should guide our belief and practice.

7. It will cause us to become spiritually mature. The prophet Jeremiah demonstrated that we should "eat" God's Word: *"Your words were found and I ate them, and Your words became for me a joy and the delight of my heart; for I have been called by Your name, O LORD God of hosts"* (Jeremiah 15:16). Jesus calls Himself the Bread of Life. (See John 6:35.) How hungry are you for God's Word—for Jesus Himself? We should grow up and move beyond the milk stage to the solid food stage.

> *For everyone who continues to feed on milk is obviously inexperienced and unskilled in the doctrine of righteousness (of conformity to the divine will in purpose, thought, and action), for he is a mere infant…! But solid food is for full-grown men, for those whose senses and mental faculties are trained by practice to discriminate and distinguish between what is morally good and noble and what is evil and contrary either to divine or human law."* (Hebrews 5:13–14 AMP)

8. It will enable us to assess our true spiritual condition and to align ourselves with God's ways. James compared studying the Word to looking *"intently"* into a mirror of liberty, by which we can rightly gauge our progress toward maturity and true freedom. Our obedience to what we "see" is the benchmark. (See James 1:22–25.) This is like a lawyer who diligently studies the law and then applies it daily in his legal practice.

As you read and study the Word, note that, in most Bibles, while the books are arranged somewhat chronologically, they were not written in that order. You may want to obtain a Bible in which the books have been rearranged to be in chronological order. Once, I spent a whole year reading only from my chronological Bible. I wanted to be better able to put together the giant puzzle of biblical events. I wouldn't want to read only that version permanently, however, because I believe it is very helpful for us to expand our exposure to the Word by reading different Bible translations and formats.

Study to Understand

Paul urged people to study to *understand* the written Word: *"I hope that you will become thoroughly acquainted [with divine things] and know and understand [them] accurately and well to the end"* (2 Corinthians 1:13 AMP). What is the best way to approach our personal Bible study? Obviously, the first step is to decide to do it. You should graduate from being spoon-fed the Word by your pastors and teachers and take mature responsibility to learn all you can. Start with the version of the Bible you find easiest to comprehend, and build your own study plan. Here are some ideas to consider:

- Read chapter by chapter, day by day. *"Seek ye out of the book of the Lord, and read…"* (Isaiah 34:16 KJV). *"[A copy of the Law] shall be with [the king] and he shall read it all the days of his life, that he may learn to fear the Lord his God, by carefully observing all the words of this law and these statutes"* (Deuteronomy 17:19).

- As you read, acknowledge Jesus' lordship. Let His truth and light permeate your darkness and, through you, the darkness of others, as Paul emphasized: *"Thanks be to God, who always leads us in triumph in Christ, and manifests through us the sweet aroma of the knowledge of Him in every place"* (2 Corinthians 2:14).

- Read prayerfully, with the Spirit's help. Take note of things that stand out, and why. It is OK to write in the margins of your Bible.

- It is also OK to underline or highlight words and verses on the pages. You may want to use different colors of ink or markers to indicate different types of themes or topics. In the future, this will draw your attention back to special verses that will become building blocks for future growth in knowledge and truth.

♦   Study particular themes, such as redemption or forgiveness. Ask "How?" "When?" "Where?" and "Why?" Ask yourself how you will personally apply what you learn.

♦   Study the lives of important people in the Bible. This is one of my favorite study techniques. As I read about somebody, I ask myself the following questions: (1) "Why did God choose this person?" (2) "What did this person do to comply with God's dealings?" (3) "What processes did God use to bring him or her to His purposes?" (4) "What lessons can I learn from this person's life?" As the author of the book of Hebrews instructed, this is *"so that [we] will not be sluggish, but imitators of those who through faith and patience inherit the promises"* (Hebrews 6:12). And, as Paul wrote, *"For whatever things were written before were written for our learning, that we through the patience and comfort of the Scriptures might have hope"* (Romans 15:4 NKJV).

♦   Obtain and use a study Bible and a concordance, so that you can follow cross-references for particular words and ideas. In this way, you can expand your outlook and gain insights.

♦   Using a concordance and a lexicon of Hebrew (for the Old Testament) or Greek (for the New Testament), research original word usages, other ways a word has been translated, and where a particular word appears in Scripture. (Study Bibles, concordances, and lexicons are readily available from bookstores and book distributors, especially online.)

♦   Meditate on the Word. Think about what you have read. The word *meditate* means to muse, to ponder, to reflect, even to mutter to oneself. Meditation will unlock the Scriptures in your spirit and enable the Holy Spirit to reveal to you the things of God. In short, *"keep this Book of the Law always on your lips; meditate on it day and night, so that you may be careful to do everything written in it. Then you will be prosperous and successful"* (Joshua 1:8 NIV).

Always be eager to enlarge your knowledge and to grow in your faith as your study reveals new aspects of the truth to you. God is so big that, regardless of how much we learn of Him and His ways, we will always *"know*

[only] *in part*" as long as we live on this side of heaven. (See 1 Corinthians 13:9–12.) You will be able to gain knowledge and sound doctrine little by little, steadily: "*Precept upon precept, line upon line, line upon line, here a little, there a little*" (Isaiah 28:10 NKJV).

Stay humble and teachable. You will be surprised at what you don't yet know, even after you have delved into the Word for a long time. In the book of Acts, we read about a preacher named Apollos who was "*an eloquent man,…mighty in the Scriptures*" (Acts 18:24). But when Bible teachers Priscilla and Aquila (a married couple) happened to hear him speaking in the synagogue, "*they took him aside and explained to him the way of God more accurately*" (Acts 18:26). He received their input graciously and modified his message accordingly. (See Acts 18:27–28.)

When you meditate on the Word and allow it to "*dwell in you richly*" (Colossians 3:16 KJV, NKJV), the Holy Spirit will begin to show you the reality of the spiritual realm that the Word describes. (See 1 Corinthians 2:9–10.) As you learn the Word and the ways of God more completely, you will be changed so that you increasingly reflect His image. This is a promise: "*And we all, who with unveiled faces contemplate the Lord's glory, are being transformed into his image with ever-increasing glory, which comes from the Lord, who is the Spirit*" (2 Corinthians 3:18 NIV).

When you meditate on the Word, the Holy Spirit will show you the reality of the spiritual realm that the Word describes.

"I Thirst…"

On the cross, Jesus gasped, "*I thirst!*" (John 19:28 NKJV). As a Man, He experienced both hunger and thirst, many times. He can totally identify with human hunger and thirst.

He also knew that bread and water would not provide the ultimate satisfaction or renewed vigor, but that only the Word of God could. That's why He told the devil in the wilderness, "*It is written, 'Man shall not live* by bread alone, but by every word that proceeds from the mouth of God'" (Matthew 4:4 NKJV).

And later, when He was again tired, hungry, and thirsty, and His disciples had brought Him something to eat, He enlarged their understanding about what could slake thirst and satisfy hunger.

> Meanwhile the disciples were urging Him, saying, "Rabbi, eat." But He said to them, "I have food to eat that you do not know about." So the disciples were saying to one another, "No one brought Him anything to eat, did he?" Jesus said to them, "My food is to do the will of Him who sent Me and to accomplish His work."　　　(John 4:31–34)

While His disciples had been gone, Jesus had been doing His Father's will, and that had meant offering to quench the thirsty heart of a sinful Samaritan woman:

> Jesus answered and said to her, "If you knew the gift of God, and who it is who says to you, 'Give Me a drink,' you would have asked Him, and He would have given you living water." She said to Him, "Sir, You have nothing to draw with and the well is deep; where then do You get that living water?"…Jesus answered and said to her, "Everyone who drinks of this water will thirst again; but whoever drinks of the water that I will give him shall never thirst; but the water that I will give him will become in him a well of water springing up to eternal life."　　　(John 4:10–11, 13–14)

Jesus is so aware of the importance of bread and water for satisfying hunger and thirst that He calls Himself the Bread of Life and says He will supply His "living water" to anyone who will say yes to His offer of eternal life: "I am the bread of life; he who comes to Me will not hunger, and he who believes in Me will never thirst" (John 6:35).

He knows how much we thirst for God, our Creator and Father. "As the deer pants for the water brooks, so my soul pants for You, O God. My soul thirsts for God, for the living God; when shall I come and appear before God?" (Psalm 42:1–2). He knows that we cannot fully satisfy our hunger and thirst until we find rest in Him.

Jesus offers Himself, the Bread of Life, in the form of His written Word. Did you know that God has exalted His Word above even His own name? (See Psalm 138:2 KJV, NKJV, AMP.)

What's holding you back? Stop everything and immerse yourself in God's Word. Give your best attention to it. Make it a priority to read it, to study it, to learn it. Give it first place in your life. In this way, you will come to know God; and, in this way, you will remain steadfast in Him for all the days of your life.

As you read and reread the books in God's Word, your spirit and mind will absorb God's thoughts and plans, and your heart will begin to beat in time with His. You will learn how to track with Him, and you'll begin to desire the same things He does. You will find out how much He loves you and what He has done to redeem you from your many flaws and difficulties. You will see glimpses into God's grand plan to cover the earth with His glory!

You'll learn how to *live*. You'll fall in love with the Author of the Book! And you won't just pick through a "promise box" of Scripture verses to get to the ones you like the most. You will end up growing in your spiritual appetite, and you will be hungry for the entire Word of Truth. "Take and eat." (See Matthew 26:26; Mark 14:22.)

11

The Uniqueness of God's Word

Over and over again, like a broken record, I hear the phrase,
"Oh, you don't read the Bible, do you?" Sometimes it is phrased,
"Why, the Bible is just another book; you ought to read...etc."
There is the student who is proud because his Bible is on the shelf
with his other books, perhaps dusty, not broken in,
but it is here with the other "greats."
...The Bible should be on the top shelf all by itself. The Bible is
"unique." That's it! The ideas I grappled with to describe the Bible
are summed up by the word "unique."[28]
—Josh McDowell

The Bible is an absolutely unique Book—it is above all others that have ever been written. It is the only Book that is alive and active. When you read it, it reads you! On our journey together, we have been exploring the way in which God's living, active Word forms a pathway between heaven and earth, facilitating the relationship between believers and their Father in heaven, noting that the same Word who has been from the beginning (see John 1:1) is pulsating with life within the pages of the Book we call the Bible.

---

28. Josh McDowell, *Evidence That Demands a Verdict* (Arrowhead Springs, CA: Campus Crusade for Christ, 1972), 17.

The Word of God is as alive as you are; in fact, the Word is *more* alive than you are! As you give yourself to the Word, you will have the living heart of the Holy Spirit beating in the core of your being. You will know God better and better.

The question is, How does this work? How can the Word make the connection between you and your heavenly Father? And how can you make the most of this wonderful resource, the written Word of God?

God's Word Is Alive, Active, Effective

Have you ever stumbled in your walk with God? When you drift away from Him, one of the first things you stop doing is having a regular time of devotional reading and prayer. Along with that, you may start looking for excuses to skip worship services, and you will certainly neglect your Bible reading. Soon you are "too busy," "too tired," or whatever. Too many people end up with an attitude of "Been there, done that!" in relation to their spiritual life. At some point, whether or not you recognize your condition, you may end up like a castaway on a desert island, perishing from spiritual hunger and thirst.

Why on earth did you cast off from your only security and guarantee of true life? What made you settle for crumbs when you could have had the whole loaf of bread? Quick! Repent of your foolishness and turn back to God. *"Putting aside all filthiness and all that remains of wickedness, in humility receive the word implanted, which is able to save your souls"* (James 1:21).

If you drift away from God, you may end up like a castaway on a desert island, perishing from spiritual hunger and thirst.

Allow the Great Physician and Surgeon to have access to your heart. *"For the word of God is living and active and sharper than any two-edged sword, and piercing as far as the division of soul and spirit, of both joints and marrow, and able to judge the thoughts and intentions of the heart"* (Hebrews 4:12). Pick up your Bible and hold it next to your heart. Then open it and read!

The Words of Jesus are life, as He said: *"The Spirit gives life; the flesh counts for nothing. The words I have spoken to you—they are full of the Spirit and life"* (John 6:63 NIV). Remember, your Bible is your friend!

Let the wind of the Spirit billow your sails and speed you away from that hopeless place. Let the Spirit take you wherever He wishes. You see, *"the word of the cross is foolishness to those who are perishing, but to us who are being saved it is the power of God"* (1 Corinthians 1:18).

Humility of heart is the best soil for the implanted Word to grow in. When that Word encounters a stony place, it will shift and soften it. You may sometimes try to twist or change the Word, but which one of you do you think will have to give in? The Word of God cannot be broken or shaken or altered. In His love, God will wait for you to respond to what He is saying to you. The psalmist said,

> *Good and upright is the LORD; therefore He instructs sinners in the way. He leads the humble in justice, and He teaches the humble His way....Who is the man who fears the LORD? He will instruct him in the way he should choose. His soul will abide in prosperity, and his descendants will inherit the land. The secret of the LORD is for those who fear Him, and He will make them know His covenant.*
>
> (Psalm 25:8–9, 12–14)

The Effects and Benefits of God's Word

The living Word will change you drastically for the better. It will introduce you to your Maker, who wants you to enjoy the journey of being recreated into His image. The Word will mold and shape your spirit and soul like a potter shapes soft clay. (See Romans 9:20.) God is the only One who has the right to shape us, and we need to allow Him to do so. Pay attention to His voice as He speaks directly to your heart and as He spells out His love to you through His written Word.

The Word will enhance your connectedness to God by increasing your capacity for *faith*. The Word will both seal your *new birth* and sustain your *new life*. And, as we have discussed, the Word will supply *spiritual nourishment* to you as you mature, just as milk and solid food nourish your physical body.

Speaking of your physical body, the Word will also show you the way of *health* and *physical healing*. In addition, it will shine its light into the dark places and give you *illumination* and *understanding*. The Prince of Darkness will be forced to let go of your life, because the Word of God will win for you *victory over sin and Satan*.

The Word is our *judge*. The light of the Word will expose your hidden sins and help you to overcome them for good, yielding the fruit of *cleansing* and *sanctification*. The process may be painful at times, but, believe me, it's a good kind of pain, and the results are incomparable. The Word brings light because it reflects the glory of heaven. This is why the Word will also become your *mirror of spiritual revelation*. You will look forward to consulting its pages in order to soak up the words of truth and the confirmation of wisdom and direction, so that you can obey God's instructions and leading.

As I stated above, when you read the Word of God enough, it begins to read *you*. Again, it is able to judge the thoughts and intentions of your heart. When your heart comes under conviction, don't skirt the issue just because it hurts. Instead, bring yourself into alignment with the living Word of God, asking for His help all the way. You will benefit when you embrace God's Word.

Naturally, people don't always like to hear this. We see a lot of Word-twisting going on when the light of the Word uncovers something inappropriate in people's lives. Their tendency is to justify their actions, which, of course, guarantees that they will remain in their unsuccessful condition. By its nature, the Word of God is not only alive and active—it is also unbending. It will not change to accommodate your "extenuating circumstances," even if you want to dress things up in attractive clothing and appeal for "fairness" or leniency. The Godhead has no faults. None whatsoever. (See, for example, Job 40:2.) God does not modify His nature to suit human nature, human cultural standards, or a particular time in history. He is unbending where sin is concerned, and He wants to "love us out of it" so that we can more wholly reflect His image.

He is our saving Lord—which means that we *need* saving. I am convinced that He is saving me daily, sometimes moment by moment, and I am so grateful for that. If the implanted Word is able to save my soul, as James 1:21 says it is—and if my soul is my "self," which includes my thoughts, my emotions, and my will—then God's salvation applies to a lot more than what happened to me once during an altar call to bring about the new birth.

I need my emotions saved every other hour, at the minimum. I need my mind saved regularly, especially after a hard day of slogging through the world around me. I need God, and you need God. We just need Him. So, I think we should receive what He sends, on His terms, don't you?

Pay attention to God's voice as He speaks directly to your heart and as He spells out His love to you through His written Word.

Let us now look in more depth at the effects of God's Word on us. I can think of at least nine specific ways in which the Word changes us for the better.

1. The Word births faith. The fact that our faith comes directly from the Word couldn't be stated more clearly than it is in the book of Romans: *"So then faith comes by hearing, and hearing by the word of God"* (Romans 10:17 NKJV). This truth is so simple that we often miss it.

Let me draw your attention to the faith part of the equation. This is the process by which faith is birthed: First, the Word of God is "released"—it is spoken, or it is read. Second, it penetrates someone's humble heart; it is truly *heard*. Third, that person's hearing of the Word produces faith. The word *"comes"* in Romans 10:17 is progressive. God's Word doesn't just land on your ear as a single blast, like a sonic boom, providing you with full-fledged faith the first time you hear it. Instead, your faith grows as you allow the Word to resonate within you, receiving it into your heart. The end result is trust and faith, which give you the ability to lean your whole weight on the truth of the Word and on the Giver of life. A portion of faith comes when the Word first enters your mind as you hear it spoken or as you read it, and more faith comes as it penetrates your awareness. As you embrace the Word, faith comes.

I wrote a book called *The Prophetic Intercessor* about the posture of faith, and it was based largely on this passage: *"Now, O LORD, let the word that You have spoken concerning Your servant and concerning his house be established forever, and do as You have spoken"* (1 Chronicles 17:23). The man who said that—King David—was not merely admitting to God, "Your Word is true." He was leaning on it all the way, in faith. Yes, God's Word is true, but he decided to rely on it in total dependence. He knew he lacked the strength himself to fulfill *"the word"* that God had spoken, so he was looking to the Author of that word to get the necessary strength. He was also adopting an intercessory posture in order to remind God of what He had said He wanted to do. Such a faith-posture produces confidence—God-confidence, not self-confidence. Still without knowing how the word would be fulfilled, David openly trusted that it would be done as God had said.

This brings us to an essential point—the importance of the action step of declaring the particular belief that the word of the Lord has engendered in us. When the faith-building word is expressed, it no longer stays hidden inside. It activates the eternal realm of spiritual activity. That's what made Mary's response to the angel Gabriel so effective. He had come to announce to her that she was to be the actual mother of the Messiah. He delivered this word to her in person. And her response? *"Mary said, Behold, I am the handmaiden of the Lord; let it be done to me according to what you have said"* (Luke 1:38 AMP). No hesitation. Fait accompli!

When you let your faith come out, your Papa God is so pleased. He sees that you believe Him and that you trust in His goodness—that you believe He wants to meet your need. Your faith is the first requirement for coming to God—and the most indispensable. Here's why: *"Without faith it is impossible to please God, because anyone who comes to him must believe that he exists and that he rewards those who earnestly seek him"* (Hebrews 11:6 NIV).

2. The Word brings new life. The most fundamental result of allowing the Word to be implanted in your heart is that the all-new, ever-new life of God begins to work its wonders in you. This life is truly eternal and incorruptible, as Peter wrote: *"For you have been born again, not of perishable seed, but of imperishable, through the living and enduring word of God"* (1 Peter 1:23 NIV).

This new life is an *overcoming* life; over time, it prevails over every scrap of your old life. John, the longest-lived of Jesus' original disciples, personally experienced the sweeping power of the new life over a period of many years. Therefore, he knew what he was talking about from firsthand experience when he wrote, *"No one who is born of God practices sin, because His seed abides in him; and he cannot sin, because he is born of God"* (1 John 3:9). The word *"abides"* in this verse is all-important.

If you continue to plant God's Word in your soul, then the *"seed"* of God does not make a onetime, drop-in entrance into your heart, only to disappear. Instead, as you abide in the Word, it grows and bears fruit, and that fruit includes victory over a constant state of sin. This does not mean that you reach total perfection but rather that conviction comes readily, with confession of sin as a sure result. Holiness grows in an ongoing way. The Word instigates a continuous process of sanctification—of being set apart.

3. The Word provides daily spiritual nourishment. Being reborn into God's kingdom means that you get to start over again. New life is, well, *new*. And, like little babies, we can grow and thrive only if we have milk, and later solid food. The Word of God provides both.

Have you ever fed a small baby? Babies are so happy and contented when they are being fed. I can remember watching my wife nurse our four children when they were little. I especially liked seeing the way they would stop for a moment, almost like a kitten purring with its eyes closed in absolute contentment, and then, with a sly little grin, start nursing away again eagerly. Now, as a grandpa, I get to watch, at an appropriate distance, my kids enjoy the same intimate, relational interaction. I think that's a picture of how we should be with the milk of the Word. The apostle Peter thought so, too:

Therefore, rid yourselves of all malice and all deceit, hypocrisy, envy, and slander of every kind. Like newborn babies, crave pure spiritual

milk, so that by it you may grow up in your salvation, now that you
have tasted that the Lord is good.   (1 Peter 2:1–3 NIV)

Five sinful tendencies from our old life must be laid aside before we
can make any spiritual headway: malice, deceit, hypocrisy, envy, and slander. Think about that the next time you start reading some nasty remarks
posted online about something and you want to add your own biting com-
ments. Ask yourself, "Is this slander?" "Does it put somebody down?" "Am
I being hypocritical right now?" and so forth. I suppose it would be fair to
say that the pure milk of the Word might just curdle in the presence of
such things as malice, deceit, hypocrisy, envy, and slander!

Of course, nobody subsists on milk alone as he or she grows up. That's
why the Word is also compared to "bread" and "solid food." People need
much more than "milk" as they grow and mature from one level of spiritual
development to another. (See, for example, Hebrews 5:12–14.) All around
the world, bread is a staple in people's daily diet. It's considered the most
basic form of nourishment. Apparently, God's Word is even more important than physical bread. Quoting Deuteronomy 8:3, Jesus said, "*It is written, 'Man shall not live on bread alone, but on every word that proceeds out of
the mouth of God'*" (Matthew 4:4).

And what does this solid food consist of? Is it only those really-hard-
to-understand parts of the Bible (those that are most difficult to "chew")?
Not quite. It consists of, as Eugene Peterson would say, "A long obedience
in the same direction."[29] Jesus said, "*My food is to do the will of Him who sent
Me, and to finish His work*" (John 4:34 NKJV). An ongoing, living relationship is implied, a relationship with both the Lord Himself and the written
Word. This Word is ever proceeding from God; it keeps on coming, wave
after wave.

4. The Word promotes health and physical healing. Something else,
according to Jesus, could also be considered "bread," and that is healing,
or restoration to good health. When a desperate mother persisted in asking Jesus to heal her daughter, even though she and her child were not

---

29. See Eugene Peterson, *A Long Obedience in the Same Direction: Discipleship in an Instant
Society* [20th Anniversary Edition] (Downer's Grove, IL: InterVarsity Press, 2000).

counted among the chosen people of Israel, Jesus was impressed with her determination.

> He replied, "It is not right to take the children's bread and toss it to the dogs." "Yes it is, Lord," she said. "Even the dogs eat the crumbs that fall from their master's table." Then Jesus said to her, "Woman, you have great faith! Your request is granted." And her daughter was healed at that moment.   (Matthew 15:26–28 NIV)

You see, God's Word is not only like milk and bread; it is also like good medicine. The best medicine, in fact. The psalmist was enthusiastic about it: "Oh, taste and see that the LORD is good; blessed is the man who trusts in Him!" (Psalm 34:8 NKJV).

From medical professionals and health insurance companies, we have been hearing a lot lately about prophylactic, health-promoting measures that help keep bad health at bay. I would say that a steady diet of God's Word should be part of any healthy lifestyle, wouldn't you? Not only does the Word guarantee spiritual growth and health and restoration, but it also tells us how God brings healing when things have gone wrong. For example, consider this verse from the Psalms: "He sent out his word and healed them; he rescued them from the grave" (Psalm 107:20 NIV).

Personally, I have leaned hard on certain promises of Scripture when I have needed to recover my health and maintain it. My confidence rests in God's very nature, which represents the epitome of trustworthiness. He wants His Word to succeed. That's why He said, "So will My word be which goes forth from My mouth; it will not return to Me empty, without accomplishing what I desire" (Isaiah 55:11). And what does He desire? He wants His Word to deliver the absolute best for His children. Let's return to a passage we read in the previous chapter of this book:

> My son, pay attention to what I say; turn your ear to my words. Do not let them out of your sight, keep them within your heart; for they are life to those who find them and health to one's whole body.
>   (Proverbs 4:20–22 NIV)

Heeding God's Word produces in us the faith to believe and to act upon what God has said in that same Word about our living a joy-filled and healthy life.

A steady diet of God's Word should be part of any healthy lifestyle.

---

5. The Word supplies spiritual illumination and understanding. As a believer, your goal is to *know* this God whom you are following. Again, there is no better way to know God than to immerse yourself in His Word, which is an ever-unfolding source of light and insight. *Unfolding* is a key word. The glorious thing about God's Word is that you can keep going back to the same verse over and over and over—for years—and it will continue to unfold new levels of revelation and to grant deeper understanding. God shines His own light through His Word. It illuminates itself to your heart and mind. As the psalmist put it, *"The unfolding of Your words gives light; it gives understanding to the simple"* (Psalm 119:130).

This effect is completely unique to the Word of God. It cannot be duplicated or replaced by a person's natural intelligence or education. The Word of God permeates you. It sheds light on your decisions, both large and small. It imparts knowledge, wisdom, and correction.

Derek Prince wrote,

Secular education is a good thing, but it can be misused. A highly educated mind is a fine instrument—just like a sharp knife. But a knife can be misused. One man can take a sharp knife and use it to cut up food for his family. Another man may take a similar knife and use it to kill a fellow human being.

So it is with secular education. It is a wonderful thing, but it can be misused. Divorced from the illumination of God's Word, it can become extremely dangerous. A nation or civilization which concentrates on secular education but gives no place to God's Word is simply forging instruments for its own destruction.[30]

---

30. Prince, *Spirit-Filled Believer's Handbook*, 66.

Derek Prince was a scholar of scholars, a highly educated man, but he knew the unparalleled educational merit of the Word of God. He appreciated God's way of doing things, because the Word not only imparts historical facts and moral instruction, but it also gives us the wisdom to make use of the information. When we walk hand in hand with His Spirit, wisdom infuses the words on the pages of the Bible. God's pure and wise counsel comes straight from His Word.

Take in the Word of God as your daily bread; let it mature you and complete you as a believer. Grow from spiritual childhood into spiritual young adulthood; and, as you abide in the Word, watch yourself eventually become a father or mother in the faith to others. The Word is your complete nourishment!

6. The Word wins victory over sin and Satan. Don't just read the Word or listen to it—hide it in your heart like precious wealth. Then you will have everything you need to gain victory over your own persistent sinfulness, as well as the devil and his schemes. The psalmist emphasized this truth when he wrote, *"Your word I have treasured in my heart, that I may not sin against You"* (Psalm 119:11).

Treasuring the Word in your heart makes it available instantaneously when you need it. This is better than having it stored up in your mind, which, of course, is also valuable. But in your ongoing fight against everything within you that is ungodly, you need the supernatural power of God, which means you need faith. Faith is a heart thing, not a head thing. You nourish your faith with the Word when you treasure the Word—when you cherish it and prize it and hold it dear. Another way of saying this is: *"Let the word of Christ dwell in you richly"* (Colossians 3:16 NKJV, KJV).

Doing this makes you "slippery" to Satan's grasping hands. When you are filled with the precious Word of God, you can elude his deceptive ways. (See, for example, Psalm 17:4.) As we have already noted in an earlier chapter, when Jesus was tempted in the wilderness, He used the Word as an effective weapon against Satan. (See Matthew 4:1–11; Luke 4:1–13.) If Jesus Himself needed to use the Word like a sword, how much more should we treasure it and keep it sharp? *"Take the helmet of salvation, and the sword of the Spirit, which is the word of God"* (Ephesians 6:17).

Again, by treasuring the Word in your heart, you can defeat the enemy every time. Paul wrote, "*I would have you well versed and wise as to what is good and innocent and guileless as to what is evil. And the God of peace will soon crush Satan under your feet*" (Romans 16:19–20 AMP). You will find it true that the degree to which you store up the written Word in your heart, treasuring it as you would a precious living thing, is the extent to which you will give the Holy Spirit something to breathe upon. As the Word overflows from your heart and mouth, the Spirit will be able to use it as a piercing sword to overcome the powers of darkness. Treasuring the Word in your heart will keep you from rejecting God's knowledge and thereby being destroyed at the hands of the enemy "*for lack of knowledge*" (Hosea 4:6), which nobody in his right mind would want to suffer.

Treasure the Word in your heart!

7. The Word bestows cleansing, or sanctification. The Word of God is so much more than "fire insurance"—in other words, providing faith for salvation and an escape from punishment in hell. Through the Word, you receive the supernatural capacity *to live above sin*. In other words, you experience its cleansing properties; this is what the term *sanctification* refers to. You get washed and straightened out as many times a day as it takes, over the course of the years of your life on this earth, to make sure you are ready for eternity with God. Peter expressed it best:

> *Grace and peace be yours in abundance through the knowledge of God and of Jesus our Lord. His divine power has given us everything we need for a godly life through our knowledge of him who called us by his own glory and goodness. Through these he has given us his very great and precious promises, so that through them you may participate in the divine nature, having escaped the corruption in the world caused by evil desires.* (2 Peter 1:2–4 NIV)

Jesus told His immediate disciples, "*You are already clean because of the word I have spoken to you*" (John 15:3 NIV), and His spoken words have become a significant part of the written Word that we have today.

Paul referred to the cleansing properties of the Word in the context of husbands loving their wives to the same degree that Christ has loved the church:

Husbands, love your wives, just as Christ also loved the church and gave Himself for her, that He might sanctify and cleanse her with the washing of water by the word, that He might present her to Himself a glorious church, not having spot or wrinkle or any such thing, but that she should be holy and without blemish. (Ephesians 5:25–27 NKJV)

God's Word sanctifies; it cleanses. Regardless of what Christian denomination a person may belong to, he or she can walk in the progressive light of holiness and victory over darkness simply by taking in the written Word of God and allowing it to become part of his or her innermost being. The Word works!

8. The Word judges us. Right before His crucifixion, Jesus explained to His disciples that, in the final analysis, His words would be the judge of each person, to determine who was worthy of eternal reward:

If anyone hears My words and does not believe, I do not judge him; for I did not come to judge the world but to save the world. He who rejects Me, and does not receive My words, has that which judges him—the word that I have spoken will judge him in the last day.
(John 12:47–48 NKJV)

While this is a credible threat for those who refuse to pay attention to God's Word of truth, anyone who hears His words and *does* believe can look forward to God's merciful clemency. *"For God did not send the Son into the world to judge the world, but that the world might be saved through Him"* (John 3:17).

In any case, the fact of God's judgment should put the right kind of fear into your heart. As the Word says, *"If you address as Father the One who impartially judges according to each one's work, conduct yourselves in fear during the time of your stay on earth"* (1 Peter 1:17). This fear of God's judgment is not paralyzing terror but a motivation to make the most of the time you have on earth to get to know God's ways—and to obey Him. The Word, which holds the final authority, is your most valuable and consistent source of knowledge about what He wants you to do.

You can have full confidence that the Lord, who loves you and who has invested Himself in creating the written Word for you, will intercede for you and help you. Along with Abraham, you can remind God of His own justice:

> *Far be it from You to do such a thing, to slay the righteous with the wicked, so that the righteous and the wicked are treated alike. Far be it from You! Shall not the Judge of all the earth deal justly?*
>
> (Genesis 18:25)

9. The Word is our mirror of spiritual revelation. Don't miss the vital link between reading or hearing the Word and actually doing what the Word says:

> *Anyone who listens to the word but does not do what it says is like someone who looks at his face in a mirror and, after looking at himself, goes away and immediately forgets what he looks like. But whoever looks intently into the perfect law that gives freedom, and continues in it—not forgetting what they have heard, but doing it—they will be blessed in what they do.* (James 1:23–25 NIV)

I know I want to be able to look into the mirror of God's Word and see the transcendent beauty of God's heart: His approachableness, His absolute purity. I want to have my ungodly beliefs exposed and challenged, because I want to get rid of those strongholds in my mind that "exalt themselves against the knowledge of God." (See 2 Corinthians 10:5 KJV, NKJV.) Even though I'm a typical guy, and I know that guys don't usually check their reflection in the mirror as often as women do, I don't ever want to stop reading the Word and holding myself up to its mirror. I know I could go away and forget what I look like. I'm sure you know what I mean!

Here's our goal:

> *Therefore, if anyone is in Christ, he is a new creation; old things have passed away; behold, all things have become new. Now all things are of God, who has reconciled us to Himself through Jesus Christ….For He made Him who knew no sin to be sin for us, that we might become the righteousness of God in Him.* (2 Corinthians 5:17–18, 21 NKJV)

In the long run, you and I are meant to reflect God's image, and the best way to allow Him to form us anew is to dive into His Word on a daily basis.

You can also "pray the Word" by applying the Scriptures to your personal prayers. Ask the Holy Spirit to show you how. You can start with some of Paul's Spirit-inspired prayers at the beginning of his letters to various churches. For instance, you can pray according to this passage from the first chapter of Ephesians:

> *I keep asking that the God of our Lord Jesus Christ, the glorious Father, may give [me (or the name of someone else)] the Spirit of wisdom and revelation, so that [I] may know him better. I pray that the eyes of [my] heart may be enlightened in order that [I] may know the hope to which he has called [me], the riches of his glorious inheritance in his holy people, and his incomparably great power for us who believe.*   (Ephesians 1:17–19 NIV)

I prayed this specific prayer over my own life for ten years, sometimes multiple times a day, because I so much wanted God to give me His Spirit of wisdom and revelation of the knowledge of the glorious Man Christ Jesus. I want to know the hope of His calling (not my calling, but His calling, because His calling becomes mine).

Don't ever walk away from the mirror of God's Word, which sheds its own light on your life. I implore you by the mercies of Jesus, don't walk away from the Word, which is the fullest expression of His life you will ever find on this earth. Let Him keep unfolding for you the knowledge of Himself that you will discover within the pages of this Book we call the Bible.

The best way to allow God to form us anew is to dive into His Word on a daily basis.

It's for Growing Up!

At the close of my senior year of high school, I was acknowledged among my peers by receiving the math and science awards. (Now, that was a long time ago!) I have always loved the principles of cause and effect. As we turn the corner on our relational quest for more of God, let's quickly review some of the benefits of God's Word: (1) It produces *faith*. (2) It brings *the new birth*. (3) It releases *spiritual nourishment*. (4) It promotes *health and healing*. (5) It cultivates *illumination* and *understanding*. (6) It grants us *victory over sin and Satan*. (7) It brings us into progressive *cleansing*, or *sanctification*. (8) It pronounces *judgment*. (9) It is a mirror of *spiritual revelation*.

I like to quote Leonard Ravenhill, the late British revivalist, who once said, "With the Word only, you'll dry up. With the Spirit only, you'll blow up. But with the Spirit and the Word, you'll grow up." Yes, it's true! That is the unique nature of God's holy Word.

12

Getting to Know God

In "beholding the Lord," you come to the Lord in a totally different way....As you come before your Lord to sit in His presence, beholding Him, make use of the Scripture to quiet your mind. The way to do this is really quite simple. First, read a passage of Scripture. Once you sense the Lord's presence, the content of what you have read is no longer important. The Scripture has served its purpose; it has quieted your mind; it has brought you to Him.[31]

—Madame Jeanne Guyon

To know God's loving heart—to gain even a glimpse of its vastness—is a lifelong endeavor that presupposes a real, personal connectedness with Him. This will not happen automatically. You can't say, "I know God," just because you go to church on special holidays and read the Bible from time to time.

In order to truly *encounter* Him, you must spend as much time as possible alone with Him. This is called communion with God. The best way to get to know someone, and this includes God Himself, is by meeting in person, one-on-one, preferably in a setting that is quiet enough to allow for

31. Jeanne Guyon, *Experiencing the Depths of Jesus Christ* (Jacksonville, FL: SeedSowers Publishing, 1975), 9–10.

back-and-forth conversation. Over the centuries, people who have sincerely wanted to know God have encountered Him in this way, and we can learn a lot from them.

François Fénelon, a well-known seventeenth-century spiritual advisor, wrote a book called *The Seeking Heart* in which he described how time alone with God enlarges our capacity for knowing Him and makes us able to receive more of Him. In it, he wrote,

> Your self-nature is overactive, impulsive, and always striving for something just outside your reach.
>
> But God, working within your spirit, produces a calm and faithful heart that the world cannot touch. I really want you to take an adequate amount of time to spend with God so that you might refresh your spirit. All your busyness surely drains you. Jesus took His disciples aside to be alone, and interrupted their most urgent business. Sometimes He would even leave people who had come from afar to see Him in order to come to His Father. I suggest you do the same. It is not enough to give out—you must learn to receive from God, too.[32]

Spending time alone with God often involves the lost art of Christian meditation, or prayerfully contemplating a verse or passage of Scripture, not only milking it for insights into God's nature and how He wants to interact with you but also—best of all—allowing yourself to actually encounter His presence.

Gazing Upon the Lord

Like a spiritual archeologist, I have taken the whisk broom of the Spirit to my collection of books and other resources to see what I could find that might help our understanding of spending time alone with God. The individual personality and set of insights of each author is unique. But everyone is agreed on one thing: It is *good* to spend one-on-one time with God, having His Word close at hand.

---

32. François Fénelon, *The Seeking Heart* (Sargent, GA: Christian Books Publishing House, 1962), 113.

Tricia McCary Rhodes, author of *The Soul at Rest*, wrote,

> In Meditative Prayer the Bible is not a rule book, a history lesson, or a treatise to be dissected and analyzed. We come to its Author with our hearts open and our desire for *Him*....
>
> Seeking God's face, we want to understand the person who wrote these powerful words. Our hearts are the soil in which the Word is planted. Every part of our being joins together to nourish the seeds of truth until they sprout and bring life to our soul.[33]

There are many valid expressions of biblical meditation (what our grandparents used to call "waiting on the Lord" and what some people today call "soaking"). The Holy Spirit has many tools in His tool chest, because the human population represents such a great diversity of needs, backgrounds, cultures, gifts, and callings. That which draws you closer to God may not work for me, and vice versa, but God knows every hair of our heads, and He will help us to customize our times with Him.

The important thing is to *spend time with Him*. Speaking of "soaking," I've always liked the way Donald Whitney put it:

> A simple analogy would be a cup of tea. You are the cup of hot water and the intake of Scripture is represented by the tea bag. Hearing God's Word is like one dip of the tea bag into the cup. Some of the tea's flavor is absorbed by the water, but not as much as would occur with a more thorough soaking of the bag. In this analogy, reading, studying, and memorizing God's Word are represented by additional plunges of the tea bag into the cup. The more frequently the tea enters the water, the more effect it has. Meditation, however, is like immersing the bag completely and letting it steep until all of the rich tea flavor has been extracted and the hot water is thoroughly tinctured reddish brown.[34]

---

33. Tricia McCary Rhodes, *The Soul at Rest* (Minneapolis, MN: Bethany House, 1996), 53–54.
34. Donald S. Whitney, *Spiritual Disciplines for the Christian Life* (Colorado Springs, CO: NavPress, 1991), 48.

We need to put everything else aside in favor of spending quality time with God.

I am drawn back to the story of Martha and Mary in the gospel of Luke. Mary refused to be distracted, even by the necessity of meal preparation for their guest, Jesus, preferring just to sit at His feet and, like a sponge, soak up every word He uttered. When Martha complained about not having Mary's help, Jesus simply told her, "*Martha, Martha, you are worried and troubled about many things. But one thing is needed, and Mary has chosen that good part, which will not be taken away from her*" (Luke 10:41–42 NKJV). Although both sisters loved Jesus and counted themselves as His dedicated disciples, which one of them do you think got to know Him better?

It is good to spend one-on-one time with God, having His Word close at hand.

Of course, there are times when we need to be "in the kitchen with Martha," as well as "at the feet of Jesus with Mary."[35] In other words, we need to put our faith to work in practical ways as we minister to others in Jesus' name. But when we find ourselves being pulled away from a close relationship with Jesus due to our work (even ministry work), so that we become "*worried and troubled*" and begin to neglect spending time with Him, we need to immediately renew that "*one thing*" that is necessary— that "*good part*" that Mary chose.

Putting ourselves directly at Jesus' feet gives us the chance to get to know the living Lord through reading the written Word (and hearing as it is read out loud). In the words of Dr. Siang-Yang Tan, "As the Spirit works, we take time to meet Jesus in each passage, to have lunch with him, to address him and to be addressed by him, to touch the hem of his garment."[36]

Another Mary, Jesus' own mother, had taken it further. Not only had she given her full attention to God's message, but she also had not hesitated to obey His words, treasuring and pondering them in her heart.

---

35. See Dr. Siang-Yang Tan and Dr. Douglas H. Gregg, *Disciplines of the Holy Spirit: How to Connect to the Spirit's Power and Presence* (Grand Rapids, MI: Zondervan, 1997), 87.
36. Ibid., 87.

(See Luke 1:26–38; 2:4–19.) Theologian and pastor Dietrich Bonhoeffer spoke of Mary's quiet dedication to knowing God: "Just as you do not analyse the assets of someone you love, but accept them as they are said to you, accept the Word of Scripture and ponder it in your heart, as Mary did."[37]

When we spend quality time alone with God, we touch Him, listen to Him, learn about Him, and always want to come back for more. We learn to give our full attention to God. There is just no better way to get to know Him! This, according to pastor and theologian Sam Storms, "is a conscious, continuous engagement of the mind with God. This renewing of the mind (Rom. 12:1–2) is part of the process by which the word of God penetrates the soul and spirit with the light of illumination and the power of transformation."[38]

Spending time alone with God is a transformative experience. Gradually, you become like the One with whom you are conversing. You can give yourself a "complete immersion" experience with God, regardless of your natural temperament or the distractions of your daily life. Follow me now as I walk you through seven practical guidelines for this kind of personal prayer encounter with God.

Seven Steps for Meditating on God's Word

To make these steps easier to remember, each of them begins with the letter *P*: (1) Prepare, (2) Peruse, (3) Picture, (4) Ponder, (5) Pray, (6) Praise, and (7) Practice.[39]

1. Prepare. Sit (or stand, or lie down) quietly to focus your attention on the living God. To begin your encounter with Him, you might decide to read a psalm, such as this one:

---

37. Dietrich Bonhoeffer, *The Way to Freedom: Letters, Lectures and Notes, 1935–1939*, from *The Collected Works of Dietrich Bonhoeffer*, vol. 2 (Glasgow: Collins, 1966), 59.

38. Sam Storms, "How to be 10% Happier: Meditate," blog entry on "Enjoying God" Web site, posted April 4, 2014, http://samstorms.com/enjoying-god-blog/post/-how-to-be-10--happier:-meditate-. Based on *Devotional Life Class Notes: Seven Guides to Meditating*, Grace Training Center, Kansas City, Missouri.

39. These steps have been adapted from concepts developed by my friend Steve Meeks, Houston author.

*You have searched me, LORD, and you know me. You know when I sit
and when I rise; you perceive my thoughts from afar. You discern my
going out and my lying down; you are familiar with all my ways. Before
a word is on my tongue you, LORD, know it completely. You hem me in
behind and before, and you lay your hand upon me. Such knowledge is
too wonderful for me, too lofty for me to attain. Where can I go from
your Spirit? Where can I flee from your presence? If I go up to the
heavens, you are there; if I make my bed in the depths, you are there. If
I rise on the wings of the dawn, if I settle on the far side of the sea, even
there your hand will guide me, your right hand will hold me fast.*

(Psalm 139:1–10 NIV)

In terms of your choice of the time of day (or night), the place, your
posture, or whether or not you want to include worship music, there are no
particular guidelines. Simply do whatever makes you the most conducive
to receiving from God. If you feel physically uncomfortable, change your
position. If your location exposes you to repeated interruptions and distractions, find a better place. If the particular time of day or night turns out
to be inconvenient, choose a different time.

2. Peruse. Take your Bible and choose a particular text of Scripture. It
should be fairly short. Read it carefully more than once. Then, write it out
once or twice. Read it aloud ever so slowly. Absorb the beauty of the words.

Bear in mind that there is a difference between *informative* reading and
formative reading. Informative reading focuses on collecting information,
increasing "databased" knowledge, and memorization. The purpose of formative reading is to allow yourself to be formed and shaped by the Word
through the ministry of the Holy Spirit. Here's another way of saying it:
With informative reading, I remain in control of the text; but with formative reading, the text controls me.

Peter Toon wrote about formative reading,

I do not hold the Bible in my hand in order to analyze, dissect
or gather information from it. Rather I hold it in order to let my
Master penetrate the depths of my being with his Word and thus
facilitate inner moral and spiritual transformation. I am there in

utter dependence upon our God—who is the Father to whom I pray, the Son through whom I pray, and the Holy Spirit in whom I pray.[40]

3. Picture. Apply your sanctified imagination and your surrendered natural senses to the truth contained within the Scripture verse. Personally engage in a relationship with the Holy Spirit to encounter or experience what the text speaks. Hear, feel, taste, smell, and see the truths God reveals.

By the blood of Jesus, sanctify your thoughts and desires. Then, in worship to the one true God, Jesus Christ the Lord, let the Holy Spirit fill your senses—your entire being.

Through this means, you can experience, with increased intimacy and power, the reality of who God truly is.

4. Ponder. Reflect on the Word. Brood over the truth of your chosen Scripture passage. Absorb it, soak in it, turn it over and over within your heart and soul. By any means possible, internalize and personalize the passage. Let the Word speak to you!

Remember the model of Mary, who pondered the word of God in her heart. Elmer Towns wrote,

> Can you begin to imagine what Mary pondered on? Just think—the Son of God growing inside of you. You feel His heartbeat; you feel His foot move; you bring Him to birth! Truly, one of the closest people ever to Jesus was His mother Mary. "Mary kept all these things and pondered them in her heart" (Lk. 2:19). She knew Him better than anyone, yet just like us, she wanted to know Him still better. Mary becomes our example of what it means to really know Christ—to come into intimacy with the lover of our soul.[41]

5. Pray. This is one of my favorite parts of the process. I take the truths that the Holy Spirit has illuminated to me, and I pray them back to God. This may be in the form of petition, thanksgiving, intercession, spiritual

---

40. Peter Toon, *Meditating as a Christian: Waiting Upon God* (New York: HarperCollins, 1991).
41. Elmer Towns, *Christian Meditation for Spiritual Breakthrough* (Ventura, CA: Regal Books, 1999), 29–31.

warfare, declaration, or even poetic reflection. I especially like to sing these Scripture-based prayers back to God. It seems to add some extra oil to the dynamic!

6. Praise. Worship the Lord for who He is and for what He has done—and how it has been revealed in Scripture. Out loud, offer thanksgiving and the sacrifice of praise. Meditating on God's Word should always lead us into adoration and a celebration of the Person of God.

7. Practice. Commit yourself to practicing, or *doing*, what the Word commands. The aims of Christian meditative prayer and biblical contemplation are moral transformation and faithful obedience. This is incarnational Christianity. (See, for example, Joshua 1:8; Psalm 119:11.)

Meditating on God's Word should always lead us into adoration and a celebration of the Person of God.

More Benefits and Blessings

You will definitely reap many benefits and blessings by engaging in scriptural meditation and prayer on a regular basis. Collectively, they will enable you to know God better than you ever knew Him before, and your spiritual growth will testify to God's transformational power.

What type of transformation should you look for in your life? Lest it go without saying, as you gain greatly in insight and instruction in God's truth (see, for example, Psalm 119:99; 2 Timothy 2:7), you can expect your love for God and for His Word to deepen (see, for example, Psalm 119:97). You will notice that your life is much more focused on Christ Jesus. (See, for example, Hebrews 12:3; 1 John 3:1.) This will turn into increased stability and maturity in your Christian life. (See, for example, Psalm 1:2–3; 37:31; John 15:4–5.) Even the people around you will see that your demeanor expresses the peace of the Lord (see, for example, Isaiah 26:3; Philippians 4:8–9), and you will delight in having a renewed mind (see Romans 12:2; Ephesians 4:23).

You may always have wondered how to achieve all the seemingly impossible imperatives of Scripture—such as Matthew 5:44, *"Love your enemies and pray for those who persecute you...."* Now you know. As you immerse yourself in the very words that used to baffle you and make you think that they must have been written for somebody else, you will derive God's grace from them.

Thanks be to God, you will now know true wisdom. (See, for example, Psalm 49:3.) Best of all, you will have achieved your heart's desire: *"Delight yourself in the LORD; and He will give you the desires of your heart"* (Psalm 37:4).

Cultivate Communion with God

Yes, encountering the living Word invites you into a dynamic process that has the power to change the rest of your life. Cultivate your personal communion with God, because it will help you to develop a deeper relationship with Him, encourage your growth in the fruit of the Spirit (your godly character traits), and unlock God's provision for you, so that you can serve Him more effectively.

Make gazing upon the Lord your goal, regardless of which devotional model you may follow throughout your life. Simply put, God Himself is both the goal and the source of our times of reflection. He is both the fulfillment and the initiator of our heart's cry, which is to know the living Word of God Himself.

It may take some time before you learn to trust that the best place to be is in your Father's arms. You may struggle with being able to wait in God's presence, not realizing that He wants to bless you, even when radical changes are called for. He makes transformation possible by wrapping His arms of love around you. You could even say that God delights in "hug therapy."

Commune with Him daily. Encounter the living Lord. He is waiting for you.

Encountering the living Word invites you into a dynamic process that has the power to change the rest of your life.

"Getting to Know You"

As I wrapped up my work on this book, I returned to my "sweet spot," which is not research but singing. As many people know, I started out on my journey of getting to know God as a child, growing up in a small, rural church. I *love* the old hymns, and I learned many of them by heart. I thought I would find one that had just the right words to make a perfect ending for this book. So I prayed, pondered, and waited for the right tune to rumble in my heart.

But I got a surprise. Instead of drawing my attention to a hymn, the Holy Spirit brought a Rodgers and Hammerstein tune to my mind. I was delighted! I found myself singing this song constantly for two days in a row. Then for a week. Now it is stuck in me, and the only way I know how to get it out…is to pass it along to you.

How fitting it is, as a conclusion to a book about knowing God's heart, to reflect on this song: "Getting to Know You"! Yes, I am talking about the famous show tune. I wish I could quote all the inspiring lyrics here, but I can't due to copyright regulations. Yet, I trust you will grasp the poetic picture I am trying to paint.

The song (written for the brilliant musical *The King and I*, which could have served as an appropriate subtitle for this book) speaks of the comfortable back-and-forth relationship that develops when you spend a lot of time getting to know someone. We have been getting to know "You"—the living God. Yes, Lord, we've been learning all about You—drawing closer, discovering what it means to allow You to be our dearest Friend.

From now until forever, we can sing of our passionate pursuit of God—getting to know Him and becoming intimately familiar with all His amazing attributes. As the song says, "Because of all the beautiful and new / Things I'm learning about you"!

This is not just information we need—it is a heart relationship we seek. It is continuing in an abandoned walk with Him, whether our season in life appears to be filled with good days or difficult ones.

To know Him is to love Him. That is my conclusion after years in the journey.

I want to walk with my Creator without shame and fear, and draw near to Him as He draws near to me. Oh, to embrace God and His Word, even as He embraces me! I choose to continue in passionate pursuit.

How about you?

~

Let This Be Our Prayer

Grace and peace be multiplied to you in the knowledge of God and of Jesus our Lord; seeing that His divine power has granted to us everything pertaining to life and godliness, through the true knowledge of Him who called us by His own glory and excellence. For by these He has granted to us His precious and magnificent promises, so that by them you may become partakers of the divine nature. (2 Peter 1:2–4)

Our Father, in the majestic name of Jesus, I declare that I want to know You as intimately as You know me. Draw me nearer, nearer, nearer, precious Lord, to Your ever-loving side. Identify the hard places in my heart and send forth Your Word, which shatters every rock. Give me a greater hunger for the written and living Word of God. By the ministry of the Holy Spirit, by Your great grace, and by the power of the shed blood of the Lamb, set me apart and make me wholly Yours. I declare that the chief end of my life is to glorify You and to enjoy You forever! Amen and amen!

Join me in the passionate pursuit of the approachable God,
James W. Goll

About the Author

James W. Goll is a lover of Jesus who cofounded Encounters Network, which is dedicated to changing lives and impacting nations by releasing God's presence through prophetic, intercessory, and compassionate ministry. James is the director of Prayer Storm, a 24/7/365 media-based house of prayer. He is also the founder of the God Encounters Training e-School of the Heart—where faith and life meet.

After pastoring in the Midwest, James was thrust into the role of an equipper and trainer internationally. He has traveled extensively to every continent, carrying a passion for Jesus wherever he goes. He is a member of the Harvest International Ministry apostolic team and a consultant to ministries around the world. James desires to see the body of Christ become the house of prayer for all nations and be empowered by the Holy Spirit to spread the good news to every country and to all peoples. He is the author of numerous books and training manuals, and he is a contributing writer for several periodicals.

James and Michal Ann Goll were married for more than 32 years before her graduation to heaven in the fall of 2008. They have four wonderful adult children, all of whom are now married; and James is now "Gramps" to three adorable grandchildren. He makes his home amongst the southern charm of Franklin, Tennessee, and continues in his passionate pursuit of the Lover of his soul.

For more information:

James W. Goll
Encounters Network
P.O. Box 1653
Franklin, TN 37065

www.encountersnetwork.com ✦ www.prayerstorm.com
www.compassionacts.com ✦ www.GETeSchool.com
info@encountersnetwork.com *or* inviteJames@gmail.com

Other Books by James W. Goll

The Seer

Prayer Storm

The Lost Art of Intercession

The Coming Israel Awakening

The Prophetic Intercessor

The Lifestyle of a Prophet

Praying for Israel's Destiny

Deliverance from Darkness

Living a Supernatural Life

And many more...

Welcome to Our House!

We Have a Special Gift for You

It is our privilege and pleasure to share in your love of Christian books. We are committed to bringing you authors and books that feed, challenge, and enrich your faith.

To show our appreciation, we invite you to sign up to receive a specially selected **Reader Appreciation Gift**, with our compliments. Just go to the Web address at the bottom of this page.

God bless you as you seek a deeper walk with Him!

WE HAVE A GIFT FOR YOU. VISIT:

whpub.me/nonfictionthx

WHITAKER
HOUSE